U0085003

Greeting Cards For All Occasions

by Jessica Chen / Mark A. Pengra

——明天就是好友小咪的生日，攤開買來的生日卡片（ *birth-day card* ），正興緻勃勃地想用英文寫些**特別**的祝福語，可是左思右想，還是只寫了 *Happy Birthday*！這兩個字。

🐌 不一樣的祝福 🐌

你是不是也有過同樣的煩惱呢？千篇一律的祝福語，連自己看了都覺乏味，又怎能讓好友體會到你的真摯情意呢？因此，我們有了出版「**卡片英語**」（ *Greeting Cards For All Occasions* ）的構想，希望透過中外編輯的集思廣益和美工人員的巧手慧心，為讀者提供一本**天天用得到**的好書。書中收錄了各式賀卡的書寫範例，供您觀摩練習，靈活運用。讓您用最簡單的英文，寫出一張漂亮動人的賀卡，隨時隨地，帶給好友一份全新的感受。

🐌 新穎實用・包羅萬象 🐌

本書共分三章，以下分別介紹本書的編排內容：

◇ **進入卡片的繽紛世界**：教您認識卡片這群美麗天使的家族淵源，領略她們風情萬種的綺妮之姿。並介紹各種賀卡的稱謂、結尾語之書寫原則。

◇ **佳節傳情篇**：本章依照年中月份的遞嬗，為各種節日，如聖誕節（ *Christmas* ）、新年（ *New Year* ）、情人節（ *St. Valentine's*

Day ）、父親節（ *Father's Day* ）……設計五花八門的問候祝
福語，為您的賀卡巧心粧扮，教您的心意祝福躍然紙上。

◇ **有情天地篇**：包羅了婚喪喜慶各式場合，所致送的祝賀慰問語
（ *sympathy and congratulations* ）。並依照致送對象身分的不
同，加以分類，方便讀者查閱使用。本章是您書寫各類社交卡片
的小百科。

　　有了本書，用**簡麗生動**的英語，表達衷心的祝福，您也做得到！
從現在起，就讓卡片的亮麗多彩，豐富您的生活空間，增添您的風
采魅力。要贏得讚美，很容易喔！

　　本書因付梓在即，唯恐有疏失之處，尚祈各界先進不吝指正。
讓我們與您一起成長躍昇。

　　　　　　　　　　　　　　編者　謹識

Editorial Staff

● **企劃・編著**／陳怡平
● **英文撰稿**
　Mark A. Pengra・Bruce S. Stewart
　Edward C. Yulo・John C. Didier
● **校訂**
　劉　毅・葉淑霞・武藍蕙・林　婷・曾蕙蘭
　陳志忠・姚佩嫺・王慶銘・王怡華・陳威如
● **校閱**
　Larry J. Marx・Lois M. Findler
　John H. Voelker・Keith Gaunt
● **封面設計**／張鳳儀
● **版面設計**／謝淑敏・張鳳儀
● **版面構成**／
　黃春蓮・蘇翠鳳・許仲綺・林麗鳳
● **打字**
　黃淑貞・倪秀梅・蘇淑玲・吳秋香
　洪桂美・徐湘君
● **校對**
　楊秀娟・林韶慧・陳瑠琍・李南施
　邱蔚獎・陳騏永・劉宛淯・朱輝錦

Greeting Cards For All Occasions

CONTENTS

Chapter 1

進入卡片的繽紛世界

Chapter 2

佳節傳情篇

Chapter 3

有情天地篇

Chapter 1

進入卡片的
繽紛世界

The History of Cards
卡片的歷史

芬芳的源流

　　問候卡的歷史，可以上溯至西元前六世紀的**埃及**（ *Egypt* ），當時的埃及人，流行著一種習俗。那就是在新年時，彼此互贈「香水壺」，做為賀禮。並在壺上刻著「祈求幸運」等的文字。這種富於人情味的習俗，便一直流傳到古羅馬時期。

　　新年交換致候語的習慣，在基督教時代的歐洲繼續流行，但要到十五世紀，才開始出現畫有聖子圖案的卡片，當時尚未大量製造。西元一八四三年，英人 J.C. 賀利茲，首先設計了第一張**聖誕卡**，並用**石版**印製了一千張。此後，隨著印刷技術和郵政制度的發達，節日互送卡片的習慣才逐漸普及起來。

　　在今天，新年和聖誕節早已成為人們互寄賀卡的重要節日。每年的十二月更是郵差先生，最忙碌的月份。他們忙著為我們傳遞祝福，而我們則忙著將一張張精緻鮮艷的賀卡，展示在桌邊或牆上，一邊緬懷著過去的歲月，一邊祈求著新的一年的來臨！

淒美的愛情故事

　　在卡片上，寫下羅曼蒂克的詞句，最早是源於基督教尚未成立以前，古羅馬的「**路波卡里亞節**」（*Lupercalia*）。在每年的這一天（二月十五日），古羅馬的男孩子，會從大壺中取出一封蘊含款款深情的**情書**（*love letter*），交給自己喜歡的女孩子，以求打動伊人的芳心。這便是最早情人節的由來。

　　但一般人所稱的西洋情人節，則是指二月十四日的「**華倫泰節**」（*St. Valentine's Day*）。華倫泰是位英勇的殉教烈士，於西元二百七十年二月十四日壯烈地步上斷頭台。據說他在殉教之前，曾經留下一封淒美的訣別書，給在監獄裡看守他的一位失明女孩，上面署名「寫自你的華倫泰」。此後，人們敬佩他忠貞的宗教信仰，也為了紀念這段淒美的愛情故事，將每年的二月十四日定為**情人節**。而華倫泰也成為女孩們心目中，白馬王子的代稱。通常在這一天，情侶們會互贈代表甜蜜戀情的心型巧克力糖，並附上一張溫馨的祝福卡。至於尚未有情人的女孩們，也可在這一天，向心儀的對象，作**愛的告白**——送一盒巧克力糖給他。不過，現在的歐美人士，則流行在情人節這一天，彼此互贈巧克力。這時的巧克力，就只代表了關懷、感謝和友誼之類的涵意。例如聰明的上司，為了感謝能幹的女秘書，可以在這天送盒糖給她。當然，體貼的先生們，也別忘了為太太準備一份禮物或賀卡，因為太太可是一輩子的情人喔！

美麗的家族

　　因此，從最早的互贈香水壺，到華倫泰的情人告別信，**卡片**這個美麗的家族，早以隨著歷史的綿延，進入了人類的生活世界中。到現在，每一種節日都有屬於自己的賀卡，例如聖誕節有畫著馴鹿雪橇的卡片，感恩節也有畫著火雞大餐的卡片。另外，各種歡樂慶祝的場合，也有代表特定涵意的卡片，例如生日有畫著蛋糕、小雞的卡片，結婚也有印著心心相印的卡片。而我們的生活，也因為卡片的加入，而變得更多彩多姿了。

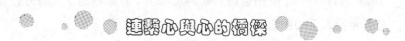

連繫心與心的橋樑

到了二十世紀的今天，人們不只在節日才互贈卡片。許多忙碌的現代人已將卡片視為書信的代替品，即使一定要寫信，也不忘附上一張精緻可愛的小卡片。有時一封簡短的祝福卡，就可以超越時空，遨翔千里，帶給遠方的友人，一份意外的驚喜。

此外，卡片的樣式也越趨精緻；一般書坊的展示架上更是琳瑯滿目，美不勝收。這些令人愛不釋手的卡片，提供了人們更多樣化的消費選擇。可別小看了這一小張卡片，在人際關係日漸疏離的今天，它可是扮演著親善大使的角色，期待能敲開每個現代人深鎖的心扉。

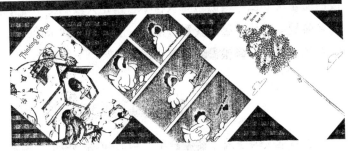

The Kinds of Cards
卡片的種類

閃耀佳節・賀卡寄情

　　歐美的問候卡，以**聖誕卡**（ *Christmas card* ）為主。但不只是送給平常少見面的人，也送給天天在一起的朋友。其性質類似我們的賀年卡。通常在聖誕節前一個月開始寄出。在形式的設計上，也以傳遞耶穌誕生的喜悅與祝福為主。不過要注意的是，送給非基督徒的卡片要避免寫著 *Merry Christmas*，而要以 *Season's greetings* 或 *Happy holidays* 代替，這是一種**禮貌**。

　　其次針對各種特定節日如**母親節**（ *Mother's Day* ）、**父親節**（ *Father's Day* ）、**教師節**（ *Teacher's Day* ）等，也有許多別出心裁的卡片。有可供摺疊的立體卡片、音樂卡片、透明水晶卡片等等，令人眼花瞭亂，目不暇給。當然，有了這些漂亮卡片的裝飾，我們的世界才顯得更繽紛、更亮麗。

　　近年來，由於國人生活水準的提高，對於生活**品味**（ *taste* ）與情趣也漸漸重視。因此，許多歐美的節日也被引進，如情人節、愚人節、

復活節等等。當然聰明的商人也不忘藉此大發利市一番，利用**廣告**促銷
這些節日，帶動了送禮致賀的流行。而對於收到卡片的人，也能為繁忙
的生活，憑添一絲浪漫的情懷，因此何樂而不為呢！

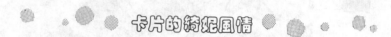

卡片的綺妮風情

　　祝福個人的卡片，從**生日卡**（ *birthday card* ）開始，有祝賀新婚，
嬰兒誕生、畢業、結婚紀念等。**結婚紀念卡**（ *anniversary card* ），除
了附在夫妻之間的禮物之外，也可以送給父母、子媳、親友夫婦等，祝
賀他們的結婚紀念日。

　　在書局或百貨公司的禮品部，陳列了各式各樣的卡片。有**探病卡**、
吊唁卡、**道別卡**（ *good-bye card* ）、**送行卡**（ *bon voyage card* ）、
愛慕卡（ *I-love-you card* ）等等。其中探病卡，是在無法前去探病而
送的卡片，不過現在也有人親自去探病，直接交給病人。其卡片的設計
是以幽默、讓病人快樂為主。另外，最近還流行一種代替便箋，可在上
面寫信的 *note card*，這種卡片可當作各種通知卡來使用，如搬家、結
婚通知、或嬰兒誕生通知。

How to Write a Beautiful Card
如何寫漂亮賀卡

一般祝賀卡

　　市面上銷售的卡片，上面已印好文字，所以寫法很簡單。只要在印刷部份上面，寫上對方的名字，再簽上自己的姓名就可以了。但是，若想在卡片上，用英文寫幾句心裏想說的話，就得用些巧思了。基於此，本書的二、三章收錄了各種項目的祝福語，以供讀者參考，寫出最有**個性**的卡片。

　　至於卡片的**抬頭**，則依照與對方親密的程度，以及寫給對方的心情而有區別。最普遍的用法是 *To* ～或 *Dear* ～。用在寫給家人、親友或女友時，可用 *Dearest* ～，這是一種充滿情意的說法。除此之外，也可花點心思，想出一些辭句，如 *To my best friend*（給我最好的朋友），*To a good friend*（給一位好朋友），*To a great buddy*（給我的壞朋友），*To the most important person in my life*（給我一生中最重要的朋友）。若是寫給男、女朋友時，這些令人心動的措辭，如 *My true love*（我的眞愛），*My foxy lady*（我的小野貓），*My dar-*

ling（我的愛人），*My sweet pie* （我的甜餅），*My sweetheart* （我的甜心），定能沸騰你們彼此的感情熱度。

一般的**結尾語**（*closing*），若不是很親密，則一律可用 *Sincerely*。 寄給朋友的話，還可用 *Love, With love, With much love*！雖然是用 *love* 這個字，但並不表示我愛你之意，而是相當於「**下次再談**」、「**祝 你健康**」之意。這也是寄給親友、家人常用的說法。若是對於工作上來 往，不太親密的朋友，需要鄭重其事時，可用 *Yours truly,* 或 *Sincere- ly yours*，等。這些結尾詞一定要加逗點，並在下一行簽上你的姓名。

正式邀請卡

做為正式邀請函的卡片，在書寫上不同於一般的祝賀卡，例如結婚 宴會的邀請卡，在傳統上是以新娘父母親的名義發出，並以第三人稱的 語法書寫，不用 *We*，而稱呼**姓名**。不過，最近也有以結婚者本人的名 義，而發出的喜帖。另外婚宴的形式也需要註明，如 *at luncheon*（午 宴），*for cocktails*（雞尾酒會），*at a dance*（舞會）等。

另外在邀請卡的下方附有 *R.S.V.P.* 的字母，是表示「**敬候回覆**」 的意思。如果上面有電話號碼，則可用電話聯絡。*R.S.V.P. by en- closed card* 則是指用附在信封裏的明信片回覆，而 *Regrets only* 則 是指只有缺席時才回覆。

自己動手作

卡片有輕易就可寄出的優點，對於無暇寫信的人而言，只要寫上自 己和對方的名字就可以，實在很方便。另外，對怯於寫感謝詞和充滿情 意話語的人，改用英文來寫張卡片，就可若無其事地傳遞您的深情。

　　如果你的點子很多，爲何不嘗試自己動手做張賀卡？我們身邊有相當多的材料和工具，只要你運用巧思和一點技巧，就可以做出非常不一樣的漂亮卡片，裡面再寫上一些全新感受的祝福語，那就更能**顯**示出您的**眞情摯意**了。如下面的這張謝卡（ thank-you　card ），就是一個例子。

　　這張卡片的製作方式非常簡單。只要摘下幾片酢漿草的葉子（或其他形狀特殊的樹葉），將葉脈突出的一面染上油彩，趁它未乾之時，**反印**在紙上，等到顏色乾了之後，就可隨意加些可愛的圖案，如貼上靈活的雙眼。之後再寫上 Thank　You 兩個字就大功告成了！你是不是也躍躍欲試呢？

● 心 得 筆 記 欄 ●

Chapter 2

佳節傳情篇

Unit 1 ───────*For Christmas*─── 聖誕節

≪ **Merry Christmas** ≫

　　聖誕老公公（*Santa Claus*）已經乘著馴鹿雪橇走到十二月的盡頭了。馴鹿的鈴噹聲，似乎在告訴人們**聖誕節**（*Christmas*）的來臨。你是不是正準備寫張卡片（*card*），問候遠方的朋友呢？如果是久未聯絡，別忘了加上一句：" *How have you been? Hope things are going all right with you.* "「近況如何呢？希望你事事都如意。」

　　一般祝福語

☆ Merry Christmas! 　　　　　　　　聖誕快樂！

☆ *Merry Christmas and a happy new year.* 　　　　　聖誕快樂；恭賀新禧。

☆ Best wishes on this holiday season. 　　　　　聖誕節最誠摯的祝福。

☆ Wishing you and yours a merry Christmas this holiday season. 　　　　　在此佳節，祝你全家聖誕快樂。

☆ We wish you a merry Christmas. 　　　　　我們祝你聖誕快樂。

☆ Happy holidays! 佳節快樂！

☆ Wishing you health and happiness in the year to come. 祝福你新的一年健康，快樂。

☆ Peace on earth; good will toward men. 願世界充滿祥和，願人類共存善意。

☆ Season's greetings. 順頌時祺。

☆ Joy to the world. 向世界致賀。

☆ Wishing you a white Christmas. 願你有一個白色耶誕。

☆ Nöel! 聖誕快樂！

☆ *May peace and happiness be with you always.* 願和平、快樂與你常伴。

☆ Have you been naughty or nice this year? 你今年乖不乖？

☆ Don't forget to hang up the sock! 別忘了掛上襪子！

☆ We've had a rather uneventful year! 我們度過了平安無事的一年。

---

good will 善意；親善   nöel〔no'ɛl〕*n.* 聖誕節；聖誕詩歌
naughty〔'nɔtɪ〕*adj.* 頑皮的   sock〔sɑk〕*n.* 襪子
uneventful〔͵ʌnɪ'vɛntfəl〕*adj.* 平安無事的

☺ 給父母親 ☺

☆ Mom and Dad: Thank you for everything this holiday season! 　　爸爸媽媽：在這佳節，感謝您所給予的一切！

☆ I'll be home to enjoy this Christmas with you. 　　我會回家團聚，共度佳節。

☆ A present from me is *on the way*. I hope you like it. 　　寄上一份禮物。希望你們會喜歡。

☆ I wish I were home for the holidays. 　　但願我能回家共度聖誕。

☆ I wish we could be together this holiday season. 　　但願我們能在聖誕節團聚。

☆ Thinking of you at Christmas time. 　　聖誕佳節，我想念你們。

☆ Best wishes from Mark, Janet and the kids. 　　來自馬克，珍娜和孩子們最誠摯的祝福。

☆ Season's greetings from Tom, Leslie and Tom Jr. 　　來自湯姆，李絲麗，小湯姆的佳節問候。

☆ A holiday wish from your son Philip. 　　寄上佳節的祝福，你們的兒子菲力普敬上。

☆ May you have the best Christmas ever. 　　願您有個最棒的聖誕節。

☆ Peace on earth, kill the raiders!

願世界和平；沒有侵略！

☆ *A Christmas greeting to cheer you from your daughter.*

願女兒的祝福帶給您歡欣。

☆ Merry Christmas to the world's best parents!

聖誕快樂——給世界上最好的父母！

☆ Season's greetings to my favorite parents!

祝賀我最愛的父母！

😊 給老師 😊

☆ Much joy to you in the up-coming year.

願您在新的一年裡，充滿快樂。

☆ Thank you for not assigning homework this holiday season.

謝謝您在這次假期中，沒有分配作業。

☆ Christmas time is for think-ing of others.

聖誕佳節是思念大家的時刻。

☆ I look forward to your class after the new year.

我期待新年過後，再上您的課。

☆ *Wishing you and your family a very merry Christmas.*

祝福您及您的家人聖誕快樂。

---

raider〔'redɚ〕*n.* 侵略者；偷襲者　　cheer〔tʃɪr〕*v.* 令人喜悅

upcoming〔'ʌp,kʌmɪŋ〕*adj.* 即將來臨的　　assign〔ə'saɪn〕*v.* 分配

☆ A merry Christmas from all of your students. 祝您耶誕快樂，您的全體學生敬上。

☆ We'll be here after the new year. 新年過後，我們會再回來。

☆ We won't forget you this holiday season. 放假的時候，我們不會忘記您的。

☆ Ho! Ho! Ho! We'll be back next semester. 呵！呵！呵！下學期我們會再回來。

☆ Christmas is a time for gladness and rejoicing... because there is no class. 聖誕節是歡喜和快樂的時光──因為不用上課。

☆ May happiness follow you everywhere... just like we do. 願快樂隨時與您同在──就如同我們與您寸步不離一般。

☆ It's really a shame we can't be together at Christmas... you must be jumping for joy! 我們不能一起過聖誕節真是太可惜了──您一定樂得跳起來了！

☆ Best wishes for you and your family. 祝福您及您的家人。

☆ *We offer Chirstmas blessings to you.* 我們向您致上聖誕節的祝福。

**─────────────────

semester〔sə'mɛstɚ〕*n.* 學期　rejoice〔rɪ'dʒɔɪs〕*v.* 歡喜
shame〔ʃem〕*n.* 可惋惜之事

☺ 給長輩上司 ☺

☆ For you and your family, boss, during this holiday season!

在這個佳節裡，老闆，給您以及您全家人！

☆ There's no place like home for the holidays.

在這佳節裡，沒有比家更好的地方了。

☆ Best wishes for a wonderful New Year.

獻上最誠摯的祝福，祝您新年愉快。

☆ May the joy of Christmas be with you throughout the year.

願聖誕佳節的喜悅，伴您一整年。

☆ Wishing you happiness now and throughout the year.

願您現在到來年，幸福快樂。

☆ May joy and health be with you always.

願喜悅與健康永遠伴著您。

☆ May happiness follow wherever you go!

願快樂永遠跟隨著您！

☆ A special card from your grandson.

您的乖孫，寄給您一張特別的卡片。

☆ A Christmas wish from your nephew.

您的姪兒，向您致上耶誕祝福。

** ───────────────

nephew 〔'nεfju〕 *n.* 外甥；姪兒

☆ *From all of us in sales:*   我們全體銷售部，祝您聖誕
   Merry Christmas!   快樂！

☆ Happy Holidays from all of us   會計部全體，祝您佳節愉快。
   in accounting.

☆ A Christmas kiss from your   您的秘書，獻上一個聖誕香
   secretary.   吻。

☆ *Your entire staff wishes you*   全體職員，祝您及家人有一
   and yours a most happy   個最愉快的聖誕佳節。
   Christmas.

☆ To Grandpa and Grandma：Merry   給爺爺和奶奶：聖誕快樂！
   Christmas！

😀 給朋友 😀

☆ *A Christmas wish for my best*   給我最好的朋友一個聖誕祝
   friend!   福！

☆ A Christmas greeting to cheer   獻上令你開心的耶誕祝福，
   you, my good friend.   我的好友。

☆ Why don't we enjoy our holi-   何不與我一起共度佳節呢？
   days together？

☆ I hope my present reaches you   希望你能及時收到我的禮物。
   in time.

---

staff〔stæf〕*n.* 員工   greeting〔'gritɪŋ〕*n.* 祝賀；問候

☆ We will be having Christmas
at David's this year.　You are
welcome to join us!

今年我們要在大衞家過聖誕，
歡迎你來加入！

☆ Take your passion and make it
come true.

發揮你的熱情,讓美夢成眞。

☆ I hope we can spend the holidays together.

希望我們能一起過聖誕節。

☆ To Bob from your good friends
at Yale.

給鮑伯—— 耶魯的一群好友
上。

☆ I hope this card reaches you
in time for Christmas.

希望你能及時在聖誕節前，
收到這張卡片。

☆ Wishing you and your family all
our blessings for a beautiful
Christmas season!

我們全心祝福你和你的家人,
有個美好的耶誕佳節！

☆ *Best of luck in the year to
come*.

願你在未來的一年，吉星高
照。

☆ The moon on the breast of the
new-fallen snow gave the lus-
tre of midday to objects below.

月兒高掛在初雪的原野上，
爲塵世萬物灑上中夜的光輝。

☆ A merry yuletide!

聖誕快樂！

---

blessing〔'blɛsɪŋ〕*n.* 祝福　　lustre〔'lʌstɚ〕*n.* 光輝
yuletide〔'jul,taɪd〕*n.* 耶誕季節

☆ With all good wishes for you.

予你最誠摯的祝福。

☆ With many good wishes for the holidays and the coming year.

新的一年，向你獻上最誠摯的祝福。

☆ *Wishing you all the blessings of a beautiful Christmas season.*

願你擁有美麗聖誕所有的祝福。

☆ May its blessings lead into a wonderful year for you and all whom you hold dear.

祝福你和你所愛的人，擁有充滿祝福的一年。

☆ Bringing you good wishes of happiness this Christmas and on the coming year.

在聖誕節與新的一年中，為你帶來快樂與祝福。

☆ To wish you special joy at the holidays and all year.

祝福你新的一年，享有無限的歡愉。

☆ *May the joy of Christ's birth be with you throughout the year.*

願你在未來一整年，享有耶穌誕生的喜悅。

☆ Best wishes for every happiness now and throughout the new year.

祝福你現在和新的一年，幸福快樂。

☆ Thinking of you and wishing you happiness during the holidays and throughout the new year.

在此佳節和新的一年中，我會一直想念你，祝福你。

☺ 給你的另一半 ☺

☆ To Mr. Claus from Mrs. Claus

聖誕老奶奶給聖誕老公公！

☆ Don't stand under the mistletoe with anyone else but me.

除了我，不要和任何人站在槲寄生下。

☆ To my dearest love on this joyous Christmas.

在這個愉快的耶誕佳節裏，給我最親愛的人。

☆ We should snuggle in front of the yule log.

我們應該在耶誕爐火前，相依偎。

☆ For this and many Christmases to come.

為這一次，以及更多即將來臨的聖誕節。

☆ On this Christmas I have but one thing to say: I love you.

在這耶誕佳節裏，我只有一句話要告訴你：我愛你。

☆ You're the best Christmas present I ever received.

你是我所收到，最好的聖誕禮物。

☆ *I only want you for Christmas!*

我只要你當做我的聖誕禮物！

☆ I give all my love to you this Christmas.

這個聖誕節，獻上我所有的愛。

---

mistletoe〔'mɪsl̩,to〕n. 槲寄生（聖誕節時裝飾聖誕樹的寄生植物；耶誕日，在槲寄生樹枝下站立的女子，人人得吻之）

snuggle〔'snʌgl̩〕v. 依偎

yule log 耶誕柴（耶誕前夕，置入爐中焚燒的木柴）

☆ Even though we are apart, you are in my heart this Christmas.

雖然我們分隔兩地，在這聖誕佳節裡，你仍然在我心坎。

☆ *I want you stuffed in my stocking.*

我只要你塞在我的長襪裡。

☆ It's sad that we can't be together at Christmas.

我們在聖誕節無法團聚，真是一件難過的事。

☆ I want to be in your arms this Christmas.

今年的聖誕節，我要在你的懷抱裡。

☆ My heart is my Christmas present to you.

我的心，是我送給你的聖誕禮物。

☺ 給情侶 ☺

☆ You are the one for me this Christmas and for many Christmases to come!

在此聖誕節和未來的每個聖誕節裡,你都是我唯一的愛!

☆ *I will be there for you always!*

我永遠屬於你！

☆ We've had our ups and downs, but you're still the one for me at Christmas time!

我們曾經共度驚濤駭浪，但在聖誕節時，你仍是我的唯一！

☆ Let's spend this and every Christmas together.

讓我們共度這個、和每一個聖誕佳節。

──────────

even though 縱使   *ups and downs* 喻人生的高低

☆ I'll be wearing mistletoe in
my hair for you.

我將爲你在髮上插戴槲寄生。

☆ Let's never spend our Christmases apart.

讓我們永不獨享聖誕節。

☆ My arms are wide open for you
this Christmas.

我張開雙臂,盼與你共度此聖
誕佳節。

☆ Here's a tender Christmas kiss
from you know who.

你的心上人獻給你一個柔柔
的聖誕之吻。

☆ I'm only thinking of you this
Christmas.

在此聖誕佳節,我心中只有
你一人。

☆ *I will never stray far from*
you at Christmas.

在聖誕佳節,絕不和你分離。

☆ I want to be Mrs. Santa to
you!

我願爲你的聖誕之侶!

☆ Here is a Christmas present
from me.

這是我送你的聖誕禮物。

☆ I'm sorry that I haven't written you, but I'll be thinking of
you at Christmas.

眞抱歉!還沒有寫信給你,
但是聖誕節時,我一定會想
起你。

☆ I hope all of our Christmases
are this bright!

願我們的聖誕節都如此燦爛
亮麗!

✳✳

stray〔stre〕v. 失散　　bright〔braɪt〕adj. 燦爛的；好預兆的

Sample Christmas Cards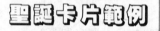

聖誕卡片範例

為您的賀卡添新粧

. . . .

Dear Andy ,

I've got a big pair of stockings.
Put your present in one and your
love in another.

Your truly loving Maggie

親愛的安迪：

我準備了一雙大襪子，一隻裝禮物，另一隻就裝你的愛。

衷心愛你的瑪姬

** stocking〔'stɑkɪŋ〕*n.* 長襪

My dear friend ,

I see the stars above to
guide us. Merry Christmas !

May

親愛的朋友：

我凝視著天上那引導我倆的小星星。聖誕快樂！

玫

** guide〔gaɪd〕*v.* 引導

Dear Professor Lee，
　　I'm sorry I haven't written
you. My best wishes to your
family.

　　　Your student, John Wang

親愛的李老師：

　　真抱歉，久未與您連絡。祝福您的家人。

　　　　　　　　　您的學生　王約翰敬上

＊＊ family〔'fæməlɪ〕n. 家人

Mom，
　　It was so nice to hear from
you at Christmas! May you enjoy
good health and much happiness in
the coming year.

　　　Your son

媽：

　　聖誕節收到您的來信真好！祝您在新的一年，享有健康和
幸福。

　　　　　　　　　您的兒子

＊＊ may〔me〕v. 祝福；願　　　health〔hɛlθ〕n. 健康

Dear John,

Much peace, love, and joy to you in 1989! Happy holidays!

Your sister Mary

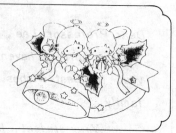

親愛的約翰：

願你的一九八九年，充滿了寧靜，關愛和喜悅！假期愉快！

你的姐姐　瑪麗

To my best friend,

How have you been? Hope things are going all right with you. Thinking of you and wishing you a beautiful Christmas season.

Jimmy

給我的摯友：

近來可好？希望你事事順心。在美麗的聖誕佳節，予你我的思念與祝福。

吉米

Dear Don and Mary，

　We wish you a merry Christmas and a happy new year. As you know, Jane gave birth to a girl last October. Both are doing very well. We hope that the new year will bring you a full measure of happiness and success. We will call you on Christmas Day.
　　　　　　　　　　　　Andy

親愛的唐和瑪麗：

　在此祝福你們聖誕快樂，新年愉快。你們知道，珍在十月份生了一個女娃娃。母女皆平安。我們盼望新的一年，將帶給你們最大的快樂和成就。耶誕節那天，我們會打電話給你們。

　　　　　　　　　　安迪上

** *give birth to* 生產　　measure〔ˈmɛʒɚ〕n. 度量

My dearest Lisa,

I'm writing this note to you to let you know that I am thinking of you this Christmas. My love for you is as high as the sky. The gift I gave you represents only a fraction of my feelings for you. I believe that we will be spending many Christmases together. I will call you tonight.

Your beloved,
Charlie

我最親愛的麗莎：

　　我寫這張短箋，是為了讓妳知道，今年聖誕我想著妳。我對妳的愛，宛如天空一樣高潔。我送妳的禮物，只代表了我對妳感情的一小部分而已。我相信我們會一起共度許多個耶誕。今晚我會打電話給妳。

你的愛人
查理

** note〔not〕*n.* 短箋
represent〔reprɪ'zɛnt〕*v.* 代表
fraction〔'frækʃən〕*n.* 部分

Dear Bob and Susan,

　　It seems that Christmas time is here once again and it's time again to bring in the new year. We wish the merriest of Christmases to you and your loved ones, and in the year ahead we wish you happiness and prosperity. We promise to drink a toast to you again this Christmas.

Your friend ,
Jessie

親愛的鮑伯和蘇珊：

　　似乎聖誕節又將來臨，又是迎接新年的季節。在此祝福你們和你們所愛之人，有個最愉快的耶誕節，並祝你們來年幸福快樂，事業成功。今年聖誕，我們一定會再為你們舉杯祝福。

你們的朋友
潔西

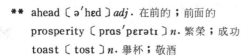

** ahead〔əˋhɛd〕*adj*. 在前的；前面的
prosperity〔prɑsˋpɛrətɪ〕*n*. 繁榮；成功
toast〔tost〕*n*. 舉杯；敬酒

Dear Mom and Dad,

　　I'm happy to say that I will be spending Christmas with you. I will be flying in on the 22nd. I can't wait to smell the smells of Christmas at home. You can't imagine how happy I am to be spending Christmas with the best parents in the world. See you soon.

　　　　　　　　　　Your daughter,
　　　　　　　　　　Judy

親愛的爸媽：

　　我很高興要告訴你們，我將與你們共度耶誕。我在二十二號會搭機抵達。我簡直等不及要聞一聞家鄉的耶誕氣息。我將和世上最了不起的父母，一起過聖誕節。你們無法想像我是多麼快樂。我們很快就會見面。

　　　　　　　　　　你們的女兒
　　　　　　　　　　茱蒂

** imagine〔ɪˈmædʒɪn〕*v.* 想像

Unit  ── *For-New-Year* ──
新　年

≪ **Happy New Year !** ≫

　　爆竹（ *firecracker* ）一聲除舊歲，轉眼又是迎春接福的新年了。傳統的中國**舊曆新年**（ *Lunar New Year* ），有許多賀歲的祝福語，如 "*Best wishes for the new year !* "（恭賀新禧！），"*May you come into a good fortune.* "（恭喜發財。）希望能爲您的賀卡，增添喜氣！

😊 一般祝賀語 😊

☆ *Happy new year !* 　　　　　　新年快樂！

☆ Best wishes for the new year. 　恭賀新禧。

☆ Did you make your new year's 　你是否有了新年新希望？
　resolution?

☆ Wishing you the best of luck 　新年行大運。
　in the new year.

☆ Good luck in the year ahead. 　新年好運到。

＊＊────────────────

　new year's resolution 新年新希望

☆ *Please extend my wishes of good luck to your family.*　　請將我的祝福，轉達給你的家人。

☆ Good luck to you and your family.　　祝您全家大吉大利。

☆ This year will be lucky for you.　　今年將是你的幸運年。

☆ I hope that next year will be luckier than the last one.　　我希望新年能比去年更為吉祥如意。

☆ Wishing you luck this year and forever.　　願你年年好運。

☆ I hope that you *come into a good fortune* this year.　　祝你今年發大財。

☆ I hope you find your pot of gold.　　祝您招財進寶。

☆ *Wishing peace and good luck* throughout the years.　　年年如意，歲歲平安。

☆ This year will be the best one yet.　　今年將是最幸運的一年。

☺ 致父母親 ☺

☆ I want to wish you *longevity and health*.　　願您福壽安康。

---

extend〔ɪk'stɛnd〕*v*. 致；給與

☆ Wishing you a long life.　　　　願您長命百歲。

☆ I hope that this next year will
be as healthy as the last.

願您今年跟去年一樣健
康。

☆ May you both live a long
and healthy life.

願二老福壽安康。

☆ May good health follow you
throughout the year. Happy
New Year!

願您今年健健康康。新年愉
快。

☆ Let's make a toast to your
health.

讓我們舉杯祝您身體健康。

☆ I hope this year is as happy
as the last.

我希望您今年跟去年一樣快
樂。

☆ Have a healthy and happy
new year.

新的一年，健康又快樂。

☆ I wish you the happiest and
healthiest years yet.

我祝您擁有，最健康快樂的
一年。

☆ You have been healthy for
so many years. I hope you
have just as many more.

這些年來，您的身體一直非
常好。我願您更為健朗。

☆ A long and healthy life is
the result of good care.

長壽健康出自細心的照料。

☆ Take good care of yourself
in the year ahead.

在未來的一年，請多加珍重。

☆ I know that you have many
   more happy years to come.

我知道您可好好享享福了。

☆ Live long and prosper !

多福多壽！

😃 給商界名流 😃

☆ Best of luck in the year
   ahead in your business.

願您今年事業順利。

☆ Have a happy and *profit-*
   able year.

願您新年快樂，大發利市。

☆ May the *god of money* give
   you a thriving business.

願今年財神爺幫您招財進寶。

☆ I hope there will be a promotion for you this year.

願您今年步步高陞。

☆ Wishing you many future
   successes.

祝你未來事事順遂。

☆ May success and happiness
   follow you throughout the
   year.

願今年，成功快樂皆伴隨著
你。

☆ I hope that your harvest
   is abundant.

祝你今年大豐收。

＊＊

profitable〔'prɑfɪtəbḷ〕*adj.* 賺錢的   *god of money* 財神爺
promotion〔prə'moʃən〕*n.* 晉升   abundant〔ə'bʌndənt〕*adj.* 豐富的

☆ Wishing you the best of luck on reopening day

祝您初五開張大吉。

☆ The god of wealth is in your doorway!

財神到，接財神！

☆ Good luck in your new business.

開張大吉。

☆ I believe that your business will thrive more this year.

我相信今年您的生意將更興隆。

☆ May your *financial future* be filled with profits this year.

祝你今年財源滾滾。

☆ Have a thriving and happy new year.

恭喜發財，新年快樂。

☆ I hope all goes well in the coming year.

祝您新的一年，萬事如意。

☺ 給上司長輩 ☺

☆ Good luck in your career, job and health.

祝您事業順利，身體健康。

☆ May many fortunes find their way to you.

祝您幸運發大財。

god of wealth 財神爺　　financial〔fə'nænʃəl〕*adj.* 經濟的；財政的
fortune〔'fɔrtʃən〕*n.* 財富；幸運

☆ I hope that the coming year brings you peace and prosperity.

希望新的一年帶給您平安吉祥如意。

☆ I hope that your reopening day is successful.

希望您重新開幕的日子，一切成功。

☆ *Wishing you a long and happy life.*

祝您福壽綿長。

☆ May you have a long life and a happy future together.

願您多福多壽。

☆ I wish that I was as healthy and as happy as you are.

但願我能和您一樣健康快樂。

☆ Your happiness is an inspiration to us all.

您的幸福快樂對我們大家是個鼓勵。

☆ I do hope that your career continues to be a success!

我衷心地希望您的事業成功!

☆ May you overcome your challenges in your business.

祝您能克服事業上的挑戰。

☆ *Good luck with the new job.*

祝您的新工作順利。

☆ I know that you will do well this year at the firm.

我知道您今年在公司，一定會有很好的成績。

—————————————————————

prosperity〔pras'perətɪ〕*n.* 幸運　　inspiration〔,ɪnspə'reʃən〕*n.* 激勵之事物
overcome〔,ovɚ'kʌm〕*v.* 克服　　challenge〔'tʃælɪndʒ〕*n.* 挑戰

☆ May you have fortune *on your side* !

新年行大運。

😊 給朋友 😊

☆ I hope you will join with me in *bringing in the new spring*.

願和你一起迎春接福。

☆ The coming of spring means the coming of new hopes.

春天的來臨，象徵新希望的到來。

☆ May you have many dreams fulfilled.

祝你許多美夢都能成眞。

☆ With the new year we have new hope.

新年新希望。

☆ We wish you a renewed hope in life.

我們祝福你再度燃起生命的希望。

☆ We hope that your harvest will be profitable.

祝你有個豐收的一年。

☆ I hope you have a happy time with your family.

祝福你和家人共度快樂時光。

☆ Please join us to *light off* firecrackers.

讓我們一起來燃放爆竹除舊歲。

**　**

fulfill〔fʊlˊfɪl〕*v.* 實現　　renew〔rɪˊnju〕*v.* 更新；恢復

harvest〔ˊhɑrvɪst〕*n.* 收穫　　firecracker〔ˊfaɪrˏkrækə〕*n.* 爆竹

☆ We hope your family and my family can get together for a celebration like last year.

我們希望你們全家與我們家人，能像去年一樣，聚在一起共同慶祝新年。

☆ Wishing you and your family peace and prosperity *for the coming year*.

祝福你與家人吉祥平安。

☆ We hope our nation will grow stronger throughout the year.

希望我們的國家日益壯大。

☆ May the people of the nation live happily and wealthily this upcoming year.

願國富民安。

☆ May your reunion be happy throughout the year.

願你們的團圓夜充滿喜悅歡樂。

😊 夫妻之間 😊

☆ I hope you will remain beautiful always.

祝妳永遠青春美麗。

☆ May your beauty shine brighter with every passing year.

願你的美麗，一年比一年更耀眼。

☆ *Your beauty is timeless*。

你的美是永恒的 。

**
reunion〔ri'junjən〕*n.* 團圓　　remain〔rɪ'men〕*v.* 停留；保持
timeless〔'taɪmlɪs〕*adj.* 永久的

☆ Wishing you everlasting beauty.

願你青春永駐。

☆ Your grace and charm are only exceeded by your beauty.

你不但優雅迷人，而且美麗大方。

☆ *I want you just the way you are*. Happy New Year!

我就是喜歡這樣的你。新年快樂。

☆ We will live on and love each other more.

我們會永遠相伴，且深愛不渝。

☆ Every passing year brings you closer to me.

願每一年都能使我們更加親密。

☆ I would do anything for your love in the coming year.

新的一年，爲了你的愛，我願做任何事。

☆ Through the years we have grown closer and closer.

經歷這些年，我們更加恩愛。

☆ On the new year, I want to say, I will love you till the day I die.

新的一年我要說，我對你的愛，至死不渝。

☆ My dear wife, I send you my deep appreciation for your patience and love in keeping our sweet home.

親愛的太太，向妳致上我的謝意，感激妳這一年來，對我們的家庭，所付出的耐心與愛心。

**

everlasting〔ˌɛvəˈlæstɪŋ〕*adj.* 持久的；永恒的   grace〔gres〕*n.* 優雅
exceed〔ɪkˈsid〕*v.* 超過

☆ I can't wait to taste the dinner you'll prepare on New Year's Eve.

我等不及要嚐嚐妳親手做的除夕大餐了。

☆ During the past year, I know you've **made every effort** to keep us warm. I love you!

在過去的一年，我知道你為了使我們溫飽，已付出一切的努力。我愛你！

☺ 情侶之間 ☺

☆ Like the coming spring, you are refreshing.

你像即將來臨的春天一樣清新。

☆ Spring is a time of renewal and a time for love.

春天是萬物更新，和戀愛的時節。

☆ I want to experience many more new years with you.

我願與你共度更多的新年。

☆ I believe that our love will grow and grow.

我相信我們的愛，會不斷地成長。

☆ I welcome spring's coming like I welcome you: **with open arms**.

如迎接春天一般，我張開雙臂迎接妳。

☆ No one makes me feel the way you do.

沒有人像你一樣，給我這麼特殊的感覺。

＊＊────────────

refreshing〔rɪ'frɛʃɪŋ〕*adj.* 提神的；清新的
renewal〔rɪ'njuəl；rɪ'nuəl〕*n.* 更新　　experience〔ɪk'spɪrɪəns〕*v.* 經歷

☆ Although I grow older every
year, I am forever young
when I am around you.

雖然我年年增長，但在你身
旁，我覺得永遠年輕。

☆ With this new year, I
promise more love.

新的一年，給你更多愛的承
諾。

☆ Let's reach for the sky
together. Happy New Year!

讓我們比翼雙飛到天際。新
年快樂！

☆ You are the most precious
thing I got this year!

你是我今年最珍貴的寶貝！

☆ You are my new hope。

你就是我的新希望。

☆ Because of you, my new year
will be brighter than ever.

有了你，我的新年將會更加
亮麗。

**─────────────────

promise〔'prɑmɪs〕v. 允諾

Sample New Year Cards

新年賀卡範例

為您的賀卡添新粧

> Dear Mr. Wang,
> It will be the year of the
> dragon — a very auspicious year
> indeed! Congratulations!
> *Mike Lee*

親愛的王先生：

　　龍年到了。這可是大吉大利的一年！恭喜恭喜！

李麥克

** dragon〔ˈdrægən〕 *n*. 龍　　auspicious〔ɔˈspɪʃən〕 *adj*. 吉利的

> Dear John,
> In the New Year, may you realize
> great satisfaction and happiness.
> *May*

親愛的約翰：

　　新的一年，願你幸福快樂，事事順心。

玫

** satisfaction〔ˌsætɪsˈfækʃən〕 *n*. 滿足；滿意

My dear wife ,

    The new year is upon us,
but you are more beautiful
than on the day that I met
you !

        Your love ,
        David

我摯愛的妻：

　　新的一年又將來臨，但是妳比我初見妳時，更加嬌美！

　　　　　　　　　　　妳的愛

　　　　　　　　　　大衛　上

To my best friend ,

    I would like to wish you a
joyous new year and express my
hope for your happiness and
good furture.

        Patrick

我的摯友：

　　祝你有個愉悅的新年，並願你幸福快樂，事事如意。

　　　　　　　　　　派屈克　上

** express〔ɪksˈprɛs〕v. 表達

To my friend Anna ,
　On this day I send you New
Year's greetings and hope that
some day soon we shall be to-
gether .
　　　　　Your pen pal ,
　　　　　Paul Lee

給我的朋友安娜：

　　今天我要向妳致上新年的祝福，希望不久的將來，我們能相聚。

　　　　　　　　　　　　　妳的筆友

　　　　　　　　　　　　　李保羅　上

** *pen pal* 筆友

Dear Aunt Mary,
　May this new year bring many
good things and rich blessings to
you and all those you love!
　　　　　　Judy

親愛的瑪麗姑媽：

　　願新年帶給您和您所愛的人，許多美好的事物和祝福！

　　　　　　　　　　　　　茱蒂上

Dear Mom and Dad ,

I will be home , of course , for
new year's day. But I want to wish
you a special new year's wish. Rich
blessings for health and longevity is
my wish for you in the coming year.
By the way , I miss Mom's Peking
roast duck and sliced beef very much !

Your son ,
Kenny

親愛的爸媽：

新年我將回家過年。但我現在要向您倆
致上我的祝福。祝您倆在新的一年裡，身體
健康，多福多壽。對了，我非常想念媽親手
做的北平烤鴨和蔥爆牛肉！

您的兒子
肯尼　上

** longevity〔lɑn'dʒɛvətɪ〕n. 長壽
Peking roast duck 北平烤鴨
beef〔bif〕n. 牛肉

Unit 3 —For-St.-Valentine's-Day—
情人節

≪ I love you ! ≫

　　每年的**情人節**（ *St. Valentine's Day* ）這一天，情侶們都會互贈代表甜蜜戀情的**巧克力糖**（ *chocolate* ），並附上一張充滿愛情誓言的卡片。您是不是正在爲這張卡片而費盡心思呢？ *" You are my fondest wish and my brightest dream. Be mine."* （妳是我最鍾愛的希望，最耀眼的夢想。讓我擁有妳吧。）這句甜蜜的告白，定能讓你擴獲她的心！

😊 情侶之間 😊

☆ I have just three words for you today: I love you.

今天，我只爲妳獻上三個字：我愛妳。

☆ These flowers are a small token of my love for you.

這些花朵象徵我對妳的愛。

☆ *I will be thinking of you on Valentine's Day.*

情人節當天我將思念妳。

☆ This Valentine is for the girl who stole my heart.

這份情人節禮物，是送給那位偷去我的心的女孩。

**

token〔'tokən〕 *n.* 象徵　　Valentine〔'væləntaɪn〕 *n.* 情人節禮物；情人

☆ May you be mine.

妳是世界上最好的女朋友。
就讓我們攜手並肩前進。

☆ You are the most wonderful
girlfriend a boy could ask for.
Let's continue to stay together.

妳讓我變成世界上最幸福的
男人。

☆ You make me the happiest man
in the world.

這些花朵和糖菓,是那位從
遠處看你的人送的。

☆ These flowers and candy are
from someone who views you
from afar.

獻給世界上最英俊的情人。

☆ *To the most handsome Valentine in the world.*

但願在情人節,我倆的美夢
成眞。

☆ May all of our wishes come
true this Valentine's Day.

這是一位不具名的愛慕者,
送來的情人節禮物。

☆ This is a Valentine from a
secret admirer.

我信賴妳。我想對妳說,我
深深地愛著妳,此心永不改
變。

☆ I feel safe with you. I want
to say that I love you very
much and always will.

妳是我心中的女神。

☆ You are *the apple of my eye.*

如果說我不愛你,那就是欺
騙了你。

☆ I would be a liar if I said
that I didn't love you.

願你屬於我。

＊＊——————————

candy〔'kændɪ〕*n.* 糖果　　view〔vju〕*v.* 看
admirer〔əd'maɪrɚ〕*n.* 愛慕者

☆ I want to hold your hand on Valentine's Day.

我想在情人節，緊握妳的手。

☆ I want you near to kill my fears.

願你靠近我，驅走我心中的恐懼。

☆ Love is all there is; it makes the world go round.

愛情就是一切，它令地球旋轉。

☆ You are the one I want to grow old with.

願能與妳白頭偕老。

☆ Be mine on Valentine's Day and grow along with me.

請答應在情人節嫁給我，好讓我們能長相廝守。

☆ You stepped out of my dreams and into my arms. I can't let you go. *Happy Valentine's Day*.

妳走出了我的夢，投入我的懷裏。我不能讓妳走。情人節快樂。

☆ Ours is a love that will last forever. Happy Valentine's Day!

我倆的愛情永恆不變。情人節快樂！

☆ I will be yours till the end of time. Happy Valentine's Day! Sweetheart.

我將永遠屬於妳。我的甜心，情人節快樂！

☆ You mean everything to me. Please say yes. Happy Valentine's Day, Honey!

妳是我生命的全部。請說妳願意。情人節快樂，我的蜜糖。

＊＊────────────────

sweetheart〔'swit,hɑrt〕*n*. 甜心；情人
honey〔'hʌnɪ〕*n*. 情人；蜜糖

☆ You are my fondest wish and my brightest dream. *Be mine.*

妳是我最鍾愛的希望，最耀眼的夢想。讓我擁有妳。

☆ Apart, we are incomplete ; together, we are greater than the whole.

分離使我倆變成殘缺的個體，祇有我們在一起時，才能結合成一個更美好的整體。

☆ Ours is not a love in vain. Remember that on this Valentine's Day.

我倆的愛永不絕望。在此情人佳節，願妳記取這句話。

☆ This card isn't much, *but it means a lot.* Please stand by me for this and many Valentine's Days to come !

這張卡片，禮輕情意重。請陪伴我度過這次及以後的每個情人節。

☆ It's hard to express my emotions and affections.

難以表達我內心的情感和由衷的愛意。

😊 夫妻之間 😊

☆ This card is to let you know that I still love you after all of these years.

這張卡片是要讓你知道，縱使時光荏苒,我却愛妳如昔。

☆ You're the best husband that a girl could *ask for.*

你是女孩子心目中最理想的丈夫。

**

bright〔braɪt〕*adj.* 耀眼的 ; 明亮的   apart〔ə'pɑrt〕*adv.* 分離地
incomplete〔,ɪnkəm'plit〕*adj.* 不完整的   *in vain* 無效的 ; 徒然的
emotion〔ɪ'moʃən〕*n.* 情感 ; 情緒

☆ After 25 years, our love is even stronger than before.

二十五年已經過去，我倆的愛情歷久彌堅。

☆ You were my high school sweetheart, and still are.

高中時代，妳是我的意中人，一直到今天，妳還是。

☆ To my one and only Valentine: I love you.

獻給我僅有且唯一的愛人：我愛妳。

☆ You have always been there for me, and I will always be there for you. Happy Valentine's Day.

妳永遠在那裡等待著我，而我也將永遠在那裡守候著妳。情人節愉快。

☆ *I fell in love with you* when I first saw you, and I still am after 40 years.

四十年前，我對你一見鍾情。到如今，對你的情愫，仍絲毫未減。

☆ I didn't think that I could ever trust happiness. Then I met you. Happy Valentine's Day, Dear.

我一直不相信有「幸福」這麼一回事，直到不久以後，我邂逅了妳。親愛的，情人節快樂。

☆ Our love grows stronger with every passing year. Happy Valentine's Day, Baby.

我倆的愛，一年比一年更堅定。小寶貝，情人節快樂。

☆ You have been and still are my only true Valentine.

從過去到現在，妳一直是我唯一真正愛的人。

☆ *To the girl of my dreams and the mother of our child*: you are the only Valentine for me.

獻給我夢中的女孩及我們孩子的母親：妳是我唯一的愛人。

**

fell in love 墜入情網   trust〔trʌst〕*v.* 信賴；相信

☆ I will be your Valentine until
the end of time.

地老天荒，我將是妳的情人。

☆ To my best friend and my loved
one; *you are my Valentine*!

獻給我最好的朋友，以及我
的愛人：妳是我的華倫泰。

☆ After all these years I still
feel like a schoolboy when I
hold your hand. I'm thinking
of you this Valentine's Day.

縱使多年已過，但每當我緊
握妳的手時，却仍有一種自
己還是高中生的感覺。我在
這個情人節，一直思念著妳。

☆ You make me feel like a school-
girl again. I love only you.

你讓我再一次感受到當高中
女生的滋味。我祇愛你一人。

☆ Your love keeps lifting me higher
and higher. Don't leave me, my
Valentine.

妳的愛不斷地振奮我的精神。
不要離開我，我的愛人。

☆ I made the right choice when
I decided to marry you. Be my
Valentine forever.

決定跟妳結婚，是正確的選
擇。願妳今生今世做我的情
人。

☆ No one has ever loved me the
way you do. I love beind your
little Valentine.

從來沒有人像你這般地愛我。
我愛做你的小情人。

☆ On this Valentine's Day, just
like every day, all I have is
love for you.

如同每一個平常的日子，我
在這個情人節裡，所擁有的
東西，就是對你的愛。

** ────────────────

lift〔lɪft〕*v.* 振奮；提高

☆ We have had our difficulties
　recently, but you are still the
　one I call my Valentine.

雖然最近我們發生爭執，但
我仍視妳爲我的情人。

☆ Please come back. I want to
　make up. I want to be your
　Valentine.

請回來。我希望能夠和解。
我要當妳的情人。

☆ To my ever loving; I am yours
　forever.

獻給我永遠的愛人；我將永
屬於妳。

☆ I knew that there would be **ups
　and downs** when I married you.
　But through it all you have al-
　ways been my Valentine.

當年娶妳，已知人生總有起
伏不定的時候。但經歷過這
一切的甘與苦，妳終究是我
的愛人。

☆ I'm sorry that I can't be with
　you on this Valentine's day. I
　send this Valentine's card to
　remind you that I love you.

很抱歉，這個情人節我不能
陪妳。我送上這張卡片，爲
的是要提醒妳，我愛妳。

😊 同事朋友之間 😊

☆ To my good friend who has al-
　ways helped me when I needed
　it; Happy Valentine's Day.

送給那位每每在我有需要時，
都願意伸出援手的好友；情
人節快樂。

---

recently〔ˈrisn̩tlɪ〕*adv.* 最近地；近來地　　*make up* 和解
ups and downs 人生的興衰起伏
remind〔rɪˈmaɪnd〕*v.* 提醒

☆ This is for helping me *prepare for* the exam. Be mine this Valentine's Day.

妳願意在情人節陪我，就是幫忙我準備考試。

☆ I really hope this card arrives in time for Valentine's day.

我很希望這張卡片，能在情人節當天，及時寄達。

☆ *It's been a pleasure* working with you. Have a happy Valentine's Day.

與妳共事，其樂無窮。祝情人節愉快。

☆ You are a dream to work with. Happy Valentine's Day.

能夠與妳共事，是我夢寐以求的事情。情人節快樂。

☆ Wishing you a happy Valentine's Day. Keep up the good work!

願妳擁有一個美好的情人節。妳的工作表現突出，加油啊！

☆ To the girl who sits next to me in class; have a terrific Valentine's Day.

送給那位在班上，坐在我旁邊的女孩；願妳有一個奇妙的情人節。

☆ This card is to tell you that we miss you at the office. Have a happy Valentine's Day at your new job.

這張卡片是要讓妳知道，我們在公司很想念妳。願妳在妳的新工作崗位上，度過一個歡樂的情人節。

☆ We work *side by side*, but I admire you from afar. Please be mine on Valentine's Day.

我們一塊工作，但我只敢站得遠遠地愛慕著妳。請在情人節陪伴我。

** ───────────────────

prepare for 準備　　pleasure〔'plɛʒɚ〕 *n.* 樂趣
terrific〔tə'rɪfɪk〕 *adj.* 極好的；奇妙的　admire〔əd'maɪr〕 *v.* 愛慕

☆ To celebrate Valentine's Day,
I am taking you to a restaurant of your choice.

我想請妳到妳所喜歡的餐廳用餐，以慶祝情人節。

☆ *I am pleased with your work.*
This card is to show my appreciation and respect.

妳的工作表現良好，我很高興。這張卡片是用來表達我對妳的欣賞與尊敬。

☆ How lucky I am to work with you! Happy Valentine's Day.

多麼幸運能與妳共事！情人節快樂。

☆ To the girl I walk with to school;
be my sweetheart this Valentine's Day.

獻給那位伴我步行上學的女孩；在這個情人節，請妳當我的愛人。

☆ Have a wonderful Valentine's Day. I've really enjoyed our long talks together at lunch.

願妳有一個奇妙的情人節。我十分喜愛我們在午飯後的長談。

☆ Thanks for helping me with my homework. Think of me this Valentine's Day.

謝謝妳在課業上，給我的幫助。這個情人節，想想我吧。

☆ You're the best English teacher I've ever had. I hope you find your true love on this Valentine's Day.

妳是我遇過最好的英文老師。我希望在這個情人節，妳能尋覓到真愛。

***

celebrate〔'sɛlə,bret〕*v*. 慶祝　　respect〔rɪs'pɛkt〕*n*. 尊敬
appreciation〔əpriʃɪ'eʃən〕*n*. 欣賞

☆ If you need a Valentine, *I'm willing to fill the position.*

假若妳心中的白馬王子還是虛位以待,我極願意填補這位置。

☆ We work so close, but I've never told you that I think you're the best. Take care this Valentine's Day.

我們工作得如此接近,然而我從不曾告訴妳,妳是最優秀的。這個情人節,好好保重。

☆ To the nicest person I've ever known. Have a truly wonderful Valentine's Day. You deserve it.

獻給我所見過最好的一個人。願妳享有一個真正奇妙的情人節,那是妳應得的。

☆ I don't want you to leave us. Please think about our love for you on Valentine's Day.

我不希望你離開我們。請你在情人節裡,想想我們給你的愛。

☆ Don't let your poor score *get you down.* This Valentine cares for you.

雖然成績不佳,也不用沒精打采。這個愛人會照顧妳的。

☆ You are my favorite instructor. I send you a Valentine greeting.

你是我最喜歡的老師。讓我送上情人節的祝福。

☆ This is a treat for you. We will all miss you in class. Happy Valentine's Day.

這一次的款待,是為妳而設的。我們全班都將想念妳。情人節快樂。

**────────────

deserve〔dɪˈzɜv〕*v.* 應得　　score〔skɔr〕*n.* 成績
favorite〔ˈfevərɪt〕*adj.* 最喜愛的
instructor〔ɪnˈstrʌktə〕*n.* 講師；老師　　treat〔trit〕*n.* 款待

Sample Cards for Valentine's Day

情人節卡片範例

爲您的賀卡添新粧

· ·

My honey ,

    A special message on a special day; I love you.

               Your love, Nick

我的蜜糖：

    在特別的日子，致上特別的信息：我愛你。

              你的愛　尼克上

** message〔ˊmɛsɪdʒ〕*n.* 信息

My dear love ,

    May true happiness enfold you and make this wonderful day the one you will remember in a warm and special way.

        Your sweetheart, Alice

我的愛：

    願真正的快樂擁抱你，使這個奇妙的日子，讓你以溫馨和特殊的方式去記憶。

             你的甜心　艾麗斯

My dearest Joan,

　　This card and candy is to remind you of my everlasting love for you. I love you now and I will love you always.

Your husband

我摯愛的瓊安：

　　這張卡片和糖菓，是為了提醒妳，我對妳不渝的愛情。我不僅現在愛妳，我願生生世世愛妳。

你的丈夫

Dearest Bob,

　　It seems a miracle that in just 10 short months my love has grown so strong for you. It seems this was a match made in heaven. You mean the world to me.

Your foxy lady,
Emily

親愛的巴比：

　　僅僅十個月，我對你的愛，竟似奇蹟般地強烈。我倆似乎是上帝特別為彼此訂做的。你是我的全部。

你的小野貓
艾美莉

** miracle〔ˊmɪrəkl̩〕n. 奇蹟　　heaven〔ˊhɛvən〕n. 天堂

Dear Martha,

　　After so many years together, I love you all the more. You give my life meaning and purpose; you give me stability and happiness. On this Valentine's Day, I want to tell you of my never ending love and devotion. You are always in my heart.

Your partner,
Blake

親愛的瑪莎：

　　經過了許多年，我對妳的愛更加深刻。妳賦與我生命的意義與目的；妳給予我安定與幸福。在這個情人節，我要向妳表白我對妳無盡的愛和摯情。妳永遠在我心中。

妳的伴侶

布萊克

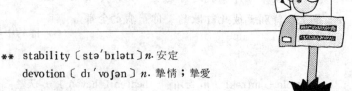

** stability〔stə'bɪlətɪ〕*n.* 安定
　devotion〔dɪ'voʃən〕*n.* 摯情；摯愛

Dear Debbie,

You have been a good friend through-out the school term. I just wanted to give you a Valentine to show my apprecia-tion. Thank you for helping me with my homework and tutoring me in English. I think your instruction has helped me im-prove a great deal. Take care and I'll see you around.

Your classmate,
George

親愛的黛比：

　　在學校中，妳一直是個好朋友。在情人節這一天，我只想致上我對妳的謝意。謝謝妳在課業上幫助我，並教我英文。妳的教導幫忙，令我進步很多。請多保重，我會常常陪伴妳的。

妳的同班同學
喬治

** tutor〔'tutɚ〕*v.* 個別指導；家教
instruction〔ɪn'stʌkʃən〕*n.* 教導

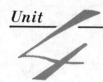

Unit 4 — For-Easter-Sunday —
復活節

≪ Easter eggs ≫

在西方，**復活節**（ *Easter Sunday* ）是指自春分三月 21日，月圓後的第一個星期日，爲基督教國家中，僅次於聖誕節的重要節日。從這一天開始，春天就來臨了，草原中百花齊放，萬物復甦，也象徵著耶穌的**復活**（ *resurrection* ），爲大地注入新生命。當天，小孩們會忙著染飾彩蛋，並互相分送做成可愛**小兔**（*Easter bunny* ）形狀的巧克力或糖菓,當然也少不了一張祝福卡囉！

😀 一般祝福語 😀

☆ Wishing you and your family a joyous Easter.

祝你和你的家人有個歡樂的復活節。

☆ This is the time to commemorate the Resurrection of our Savior.

這是紀念我們的救世主，再復活的時刻。

☆ We invite you to join us for Easter and an Easter egg hunt!

我們邀請您一起歡度復活節，參加復活節獵尋彩蛋活動。

☆ *Here is an Easter surprise from someone who loves you.*

這是一份復活節的驚喜。來自於愛你的人。

＊＊

commemorate〔kə'mɛmə,ret〕*v.* 紀念

☆ Easter is a time for love
and understanding.

復活節是個關愛與諒解的時
刻。

☆ The rabbit and the egg are
symbols of love and life.
From our family to your
family we wish a happy
Easter.

兔子和彩蛋是愛與生命的象
徵。我們全家人祝福你們有
個快樂的復活節。

☆ It's spring and the clover
is out. This is the time
for everyone to celebrate
Easter and Christ's Resurrection.

春天到了，苜蓿開徧原野。
這是每個人慶祝復活節和耶
穌復活的時刻。

☆ Life is brighter, hearts are
lighter. Winter is over,
we're all in clover.

生活更加亮麗，心情更加輕
鬆。冬天結束了，我們生活
在徧開的苜蓿中。

☆ To my loving parents at
Easter.

在復活節這一天，給我親愛
的爸媽。

☆ To our wonderful son with
love and pride at Easter.

在復活節這一天，以慈愛和
驕傲的心情,給我最棒的兒子。

☆ With Easter upon us, it is
a time to think about why
Jesus died and was reborn.
He died for your sins and
your love.

復活節的來臨，正好讓我們
思考耶穌爲何死而復活。祂
是爲了你的罪和愛而死。

☆ Easter is too important to let pass so quickly.

復活節如此重要，可別讓它匆匆過去喔！

☆ *During the Easter Week, we should all reflect upon all the goodness that the Lord has given us.*

在復活節這個星期，我們應該感念上帝所賜予的恩惠。

☆ In this time of Lent, we fast and do penitence just as Jesus did. Soon we will celebrate his resurrection. Oh, what a joyous time it will be.

在四旬齋戒期中，我們和耶穌一樣絕食和懺悔。現在，我們就要慶祝祂的復活了。噢！那將是多麼歡樂的時刻。

☆ It is a shame that such an important holiday passes so quickly.

眞可惜！這麼重要的節日這麼快就過去了。

☆ To our wonderful grandson at this special time of the year.

在一年中，這個特別的日子，給我們最乖的孫子。

☆ *An Easter wish from me to you.*

致上一份復活節的祝福。

☆ There is no better time than Easter to say I love you.

沒有比復活節更適合讓我對你說聲我愛你。

Lent〔lɛnt〕*n.* 四旬齋（以 Ash Wednesday 至 Easter Eve 的 40 天爲期；爲紀念耶穌在荒郊禁食而行絕食或懺悔）

☆ No one could be as lucky as me to have such wonderful parents. Happy Easter.

沒有人能像我這麼幸運,擁有這麼棒的爸媽。復活節快樂。

☆ Easter is a time for reflection. We ought to think about how lucky we are to have so many that love us. This is a joyous time indeed.

復活節是個內省的時刻。我們該想到我們是多麼幸運,能擁有這麼多人的愛。這真是個歡愉的日子。

☆ An Easter-time Hi !

復活節的問候!

☆ An Easter note from someone who loves you.

一封復活節的問候短箋,來自愛你的人。

☆ An Easter note across the miles.

一張越過千山萬水的復活節祝福卡。

☆ *Happy Easter, with loving memories.*

願你擁有美好的回憶;復活節快樂。

☆ Wishing you a wonderful Easter. I hope to see you in a few short weeks.

祝你有個愉快的復活節。希望在短短的幾個星期後,能見到你。

＊＊────────────

reflection〔rɪˊflɛkʃən〕*n.* 內省   Easter〔ˊistɚ〕*n.* 復活節
note〔not〕*n.* 短箋;便條

Sample Cards for Easter

復活節賀卡範例

爲您的賀卡添新粧

To my lovely Jennifer,
　　It was such a good Friday,
I hope your Easter Sunday goes
well too.

Alice

我可愛的珍妮佛：

　　這是個美好的星期五，希望妳的復活節一樣美好。

艾麗斯

Dear Don and Carol,
　　What a joyous time this is
for our family！We hope that
your Easter is equally as joyous.

Your friend

親愛的唐和凱若爾：

　　對我們家人而言，這是一個歡樂的時刻！希望你們的復活節也一樣充滿歡樂。

你們的朋友　上

** joyous〔'dʒɔɪəs〕*adj.* 歡樂的

Dear Mom and Dad,

I'm writing to wish you both a happy Easter. This is the time to think about all those who love you. I wish I could be there for this year's Easter dinner, but it's hard to get away from work. I'm sending along an Easter Bunny for you to enjoy after the dinner.

Your son
Joe

親愛的爸媽：

祝您倆有個快樂的復活節。這是個思念所有深愛您倆的人的時刻。我真希望能與你們共進復活節大餐，但是工作卻令我分不開身。因此我將送你們一盒糖菓，讓你們做為餐後甜點。

你們的兒子
喬

** **Easter Bunny** 做成兔子形狀的糖菓（多在復活節時致送）

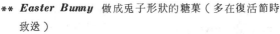

Unit **5** ———*For Mother's Day*———
母親節

≪ **Happy Mother's Day** ≫

「上帝無法照顧到世界上全部的人，所以祂創造了**母親**。」
古今中外，歌頌母親慈愛的詩篇，不知有多少。即使一張小小
的賀卡，無法表達我們對母親感激的千萬分之一，但是一句發
自內心的感言：***"Having you for a mommy is more fun
than playing hide and seek and watching cartoons."*** （有
您這樣的媽咪，要比玩捉迷藏和看卡通，好玩多了。）却是母
親們最大的安慰了。

😊 **給母親** 😊

☆ To the world's ***number one mom***! 　　給世界上最好的媽媽！

☆ You are the best mom that a
son ever had.
您是兒子心目中，最好的媽
媽。

☆ Here's a little token of my appreciation for all that you have
done for me over the years.
這是我一點小小的心意，感
謝您這麼多年來，所付出的
一切。

☆ Sometimes it may not seem like
it, but I really do love you.
有時候也許好像不是這樣，
但是我眞的愛您。

----
token〔'tokən〕*n.* 心意；象徵

☆ There may be moms all over Taiwan, but you're the only one that matters to me.

全台灣也許到處都有媽媽，但您是我唯一最在意的。

☆ I want to wish you a happy Mother's Day.

祝福您母親節快樂。

☆ *Thank you for everything over the years*, mom.

媽媽，謝謝您這些年來所做的一切。

☆ Moms should get more than a special day, they should get a medal of honor.

媽媽們應該得到的不只是一個節日，她們該獲得榮譽勳章。

☆ Mother's Day is a time when mothers discover how well their children can prepare breakfast.

母親節是媽媽們發現，她們的小孩，會把早餐做得多好的時刻。

☆ Considering the quality of food that children make their mothers on Mother's Day, it becomes apparent that without moms, their kids would *starve to death*.

想想母親節時，孩子們為媽媽所做的早餐；很明顯的，如果沒有媽媽，孩子們將會餓死。

☆ We would love to fix breakfast for you mom, but we think it would be safer for us all if we took you out.

媽媽，我們很樂意為您準備早餐，不過我們想如果帶您上館子，會比較保險一點。

---

medal〔'mɛdḷ〕*n.* 獎章；勳章　　discover〔dɪs'kʌvɚ〕*v.* 發現

apparent〔ə'pɛrənt〕*adj.* 明顯的　　starve〔stɑrv〕*v.* 飢餓

☆ This card is to let you know that *you have done a super job raising us children*.

這張卡片，是想告訴您，在教養子女方面，您做得棒極了。

☆ When I was sick, you always stood by me.

當我生病時，您總是陪伴著我。

☆ This is the day that we appreciate all the things that moms do for us. Thank you.

在這個日子裡，我們感謝媽媽為我們所做的一切。謝謝您。

☆ Roses are red, violets are blue. This card on Mother's Day is especially for you.

玫瑰是紅色的，紫羅蘭是藍色的。這張母親卡是特別給您的。

☆ We may not be angels all of the time, but we do appreciate what you do.

我們也許不是一直都像天使那樣乖巧，但我們確實感激您的教誨。

☆ Thanks for being there, mom. Happy Mother's Day.

謝謝您不斷地扶持我。祝您母親節快樂。

☆ This card comes from the whole family. Happy Mother's Day.

這張卡片是我們全家合送的。祝您母親節快樂。

☆ Today is your day to relax and let us take care of you. *Happy Mother's Day*.

今天是您休息的日子，讓我們來照顧您。母親節快樂。

**

raise〔rez〕*v.* 教養　　violet〔'vaɪəlɪt〕*n.* 紫羅蘭

angel〔'endʒəl〕*n.* 天使　　relax〔rɪ'læks〕*v.* 休息

☆ We will try to *make this your best* Mother's Day ever.

我們將努力，使今天成爲您過得最愉快的母親節。

☆ On this day we honor you, dear mother.

親愛的媽媽，我們向您致敬。

☆ Where would we be without you, mom?

媽媽，沒有您我們將流落何方呢？

☆ On this day we all sit back and think about how much our mothers do for us.

在這一天，我們將會抽空休息一下，想想媽媽們幫我們做了多少事。

☆ I've tried many times to tell you, but I'll say it again: I love you mother.

我已經告訴您許多次了，但是我將再說一次：我愛您，媽媽。

☆ Though it is hard to tell you sometimes, I do love you dearly, mom.

雖然有時要告訴您，並不太容易，但是我眞的非常愛您，媽媽。

☆ *I may not often say it, but I do love you.*

我也許並不常掛在嘴上，但我眞正愛您。

☆ There are little things that I should have said and done to show my gratitude, but it is appreciated what you do.

雖然表示謝意，我說的和做的都那麼少，但却都是感激您所做的一切。

---

sit back （背靠椅子而）坐；休息

gratitude〔'grætə,tjud〕*n.* 感激；謝意

☆ I don't take the time to tell you this often, but I love you, mom.

雖然我經常沒有時間告訴您，但我真的愛您，媽媽。

☆ Sometimes I cry and make you sigh, but you know that I love you so.

有時候我哭泣而使您嘆息，但您却知道，我是如此地愛您。

☆ To mother on Mother's Day: Thank you for all of the wonderful things that you have done for me.

母親節給媽媽：謝謝您，為我做了那麼多奇妙的事。

☆ This card is from all of us. It may not be the greatest, but it's from the heart.

這張卡片是我們合送的。它也許不是最棒的，但却是出自內心的。

☆ Mother, I just want to let you know that you are always in my thoughts.

媽媽，我只是想讓您知道，您一直都在我的心中。

☆ On this Mother's Day I just want to say: *I'm proud to be your daughter*.

在這個母親節裡，我只是想說：我以身為您的女兒為榮。

☆ To the most patient and understanding person I know. Thanks for being there. Happy Mother's Day.

給我所知道，最有耐心，最明理的人。謝謝您一直在那裡支持我。母親節快樂。

**

sign〔saɪŋ〕v. 嘆息　　patient〔'peʃənt〕adj. 有耐心的

☆ I will be thinking of you on this Mother's Day. Thanks, mom.

在母親節裡，我會一直想念著您。謝謝媽媽。

☆ We all love you very much, mom.

媽媽，我們都非常地愛您。

☆ I just put a gift into the mail. I hope it reaches you *in time* for Mother's Day. Have a very happy Mother's Day. I wish I could be there to share it with you.

我剛剛郵寄了一份禮物。希望它能趕上母親節到您手上。祝您有一個很快樂的母親節。我希望能在那邊與您一起分享。

☆ We found out in life that there are three kinds of law: state law, federal law and Mom's law. Thanks for keeping us *out of trouble*. Happy Mother's Day.

我們發現，在生命中有三種法律：州法、聯邦法和母親的法律。謝謝您，使我們遠離麻煩。母親節快樂。

☆ We wish you the best of health on this Mother's Day.

在母親節，我們祝福您身體健康。

☆ What luck! This year your birthday and Mother's Day are on the same day. This *calls for* a double celebration.

真幸運！今年您的生日和母親節是同一天。這需要雙重慶祝。

**

share〔∫ɛr〕*v.* 分享　　***federal law*** 聯邦法律
out of trouble 遠離麻煩　　***call for*** 需要

☆ Having you for a mom is more fun than watching TV or bouncing on the bed.

有您當媽媽，比看電視或跳彈簧床好玩多了。

☆ When you are sick, it's real hard to be a mommy for a mommy. That's how I know you do is real hard. Thank you.

當您生病時，我要當媽咪照顧媽咪，可真是難。那時我才知道，您做的真是不容易。謝謝您。

☆ This card is *a token of my love* for the dearest mother in the world.

這張卡片，代表著我對世上最敬愛的母親所有的愛。

☆ Mom, thank you for being you.

媽媽，謝謝您的一切。

☆ Since you have spent so much time taking care of us, we want to take care of you today. Happy Mother's Day.

由於您花費那麼多的時間照顧我們，我們今天要照顧您。母親節快樂。

☆ You are the one that we love the most. Have a happy Mother's Day.

您是我們最愛的人。祝您有一個快樂的母親節。

☆ I appreciate you all year round, but today I really want to show my love.

整年我都感激著您，但是今天，我要真正地把我的愛表示出來。

⁎⁎────────────────────

bounce〔baʊns〕*v.* 跳躍

☆ No other mom could be a mother like you are.

没有別的母親能像您這樣。

☆ Since we have faces that only a mother could love, we sure are glad that you are our mother. Happy Mother's Day.

由於我們長著只有一位母親才會愛的臉孔，我們很高興您是我們的母親。母親節快樂。

☆ *Take good care of yourself.* We all love you, mom.

請好好地照顧自己。我們都愛您，媽媽。

☆ Mom, today you are not to move a muscle. We are all *at your beck and call.*

媽，今天您連動也不用動一下。我們全體都聽您指揮。

☺ 給祖母 ☺

☆ You are the nicest Grandma in the whole world.

您是全世界最好的奶奶。

☆ I send this card with love to you, Grandma, who's always so gracious.

我愛您，奶奶，您總是那麼慈祥。

☆ *This card is especially for Grandma on Mother's Day.*

在母親節，這張卡片是特別給奶奶的。

☆ Next to mom, you are my favorite lady. Happy Mother's Day.

除了媽以外，您是我最敬愛的女士。母親節快樂。

✷✷

muscle〔'mʌsḷ〕*n*. 肌肉　　*beck and call* 聽從指揮

☆ Thank you for being such a wonderful Grandma.

謝謝您，讓我有一個這麼好的祖母。

☆ I made this card for you, Nanna, on Mother's Day.

奶奶，在母親節裡，我特別為您做了這張卡片。

☆ This card is a big kiss for you on Mother's Day.

這張卡片，是我送給您，母親節一個大大的香吻。

☆ Wishing you *the best of health* on this Mother's Day.

祝福您母親節身體健康。

☆ I hope that you will come down and see us sometime. We miss you. Have a happy Mother's Day.

希望您有空能來看看我們。我們想念您。祝您有一個愉快的母親節。

☆ It's been so long since we've gotten together. Here's a little card to let you know that you're in our thoughts often.

自從我們上次見面以後，已經又過了很久了。這一張小小的卡片，是想讓您知道，您一直都在我們的腦海裡。

☆ Thank you for your love and care over the years. It's appreciated.

感謝您這些年來的關愛和照顧。謝謝您。

☆ *Even though* it is not often said, I am always grateful to you.

雖然並不常常掛在嘴邊，但我一直深深地感謝著您。

---

grateful〔ˈgretfəl〕*adj.* 感激的

☆ It was nice talking to you on the telephone *the other day.* This card is to show that we still care. Happy Mother's Day.

前幾天跟您通電話眞好。這張卡片是告訴您，我們仍然想念您。母親節快樂。

☆ All my love to the dearest grandmother in the world.

獻上我所有的愛，給世界上我最親愛的祖母。

☆ We may live a long way from one another, but our hearts are *as close as ever.*

我們也許遠隔天邊，但是我們的心却永遠相通。

☆ This card comes from the whole family. Happy Mother's Day.

這張卡片是我們全家合送的。母親節快樂。

☆ It's your day to relax and let Grandpa *take care* of you.

今天是您休息的日子，讓爺爺好好照顧您。

☆ Grandma, I'm proud to be your grandson.

奶奶，我以身爲您的孫子爲榮。

☆ You've been a number one Grandma over the years. Happy Mother's Day.

這些年來，您都是天下第一好的奶奶。母親節快樂。

☆ You may not be my mother, but you are a mother nonetheless. Here's a Mother's Day card for you.

您雖然不是我媽媽，但您仍然是一位媽媽。這張母親卡獻給您。

**

nonetheless 〔͵nʌnðə'lɛs〕 *adv.* 仍然

☆ Mother's Day is to honor all mothers, not just your own. Happy Mother's Day Grandma.

母親節是爲了向所有的母親致敬，而非只是自己的母親。母親節快樂，奶奶

☆ Without Grandmas, mamas wouldn't be possible. Thank you Grandma.

沒有奶奶，就不會有媽媽。謝謝您，奶奶。

☆ We don't see each other often, but you are close to my heart. Have a wonderful Mother's day, Grandma.

我們雖然不常見面，但是您一直在我心底。祝您有一個愉快的母親節，奶奶。

☆ We will take care of you on Mother's Day. That's to make up for all of the care you have given us.

在母親節時，我們將會照顧您。這是爲了報答您給我們這麼多的照顧。

☆ To the world's number one Grandma.

給全天下最棒的奶奶。

☆ Thank you for everything *over the years*, Grandma.

奶奶，謝謝您這些年來所做的一切。

☆ Thanks for being there, Grandma.

奶奶，謝謝您一直在那裡照顧我。

☆ What you do, you do better than any other Grandma. Happy Mother's Day.

不論您做什麼，您做得比其它的奶奶都好。母親節快樂。

☆ *Roses are red, violets are blue.* This card's for you Grandma because I love you.

玫瑰是紅色的，紫羅蘭是藍色的。奶奶，這張卡片是給您的，因爲我愛您。

☆ This Mother's Day card is a token of　my love for you, Grandma.

奶奶，這張母親卡是我愛您的象徵。

☆ Grandma, I can't forget your delicious apple-pie.　Happy Mother's Day.

奶奶，我忘不了您做的可口蘋果派。母親節快樂。

☆ We offer you our sincerest wishes for a very enjoyable Mother's Day.

我們誠摯地祝福您母親節愉快。

＊＊

delicious〔dɪ'lɪʃəs〕*adj.* 美味可口的
enjoyable〔ɪn'dʒɔɪəbl̩〕*adj.* 愉快的

Sample Cards for Mother's Day

母親節卡片範例

為您的賀卡添新粧

Dear Mommy,
    It's because of your never-ending devotion, we all love you very much.

        Your three sons,
        Jack, Joe and Tom

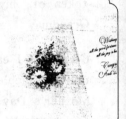

親愛的媽咪：

因為您無盡的付出，我們都非常愛您。

您的三個兒子

傑克，喬和湯姆　敬上

** devotion〔dɪ'voʃən〕 *n.* 付出；獻身

Mom,
    Because today is your special day, we are all taking you out to dinner at your favorite restaurant!
    Dad, and your daughters

媽：

因為今天是屬於您的日子，我們將帶您去您最喜愛的餐廳，大吃一頓！

爸地和您的女兒們　上

Dear Mom,

We take time out on this special day to honor you. It's because of your love, patience and understanding over the years. Happy Mother's Day!

Your son, Bill

親愛的媽媽：

在這個特別的日子，我們向您致上敬意。這是因為您多年來的關愛、耐心和體諒。母親節快樂！

您的兒子比爾

** honor 〔'hɑnɚ〕 v. 致上敬意
understanding 〔͵ʌndɚ'stændɪŋ〕 n. 體諒

Dear Mom,

　　Happy Mother's Day. We are not a very open family in some ways. It's hard for us to say it sometimes, but it's true that we all love you very much.

Doris & Judy

親愛的媽媽：

　　母親節快樂。我們並不是一個很開放的家庭。有時要我們開口實在很難，但是我們都非常愛您。

桃麗絲和茱蒂

Dear Mom,

I am sorry that I cannot be there on Mother's Day. I am just too busy at work these days. I hope that you like the flowers that I sent. They are only a small token of my appreciation. I love you mom. I'll call you this weekend.

Your son,
Neil

親愛的媽媽：

很抱歉我母親節無法回家。因為這些日子，工作太過忙碌。希望您會喜歡我送的花。它們只是表示我感激的一點小心意。我愛您，媽。這個週末我會打電話給您。

您的兒子
尼爾

Dear Grandma,

I'm writing to wish you a happy Mother's Day. You have been so nice to all of us over the years. I think that you are the world's number one grandma. So I send this card to you on this special day. Happy Mother's Day again!

Your loving grandson,
Philip

親愛的奶奶：

寫這張卡片，祝您有一個快樂的母親節。這些年來，您對我們大家都這麼好。我想您是世界最好的奶奶了。所以，在這個特別的日子裡，我寄上這張卡片。再次祝您母親節愉快！

您的乖孫
菲力普　上

Unit 6 ─ For-Father's-Day ─
父親節

≪ I love you, Dad. ≫

我們常常歌頌母親的偉大，但是可別忘了終年在外辛苦工作的**父親**喔！或許您的爸爸有些嚴肅，又或許您常惹他生氣，也可能您羞於表白自己的情感。那麼用英文寫張祝福卡，是最合適不過了。"*It is sometimes hard to say, but I am grateful for what you have done.*"（雖然有時很難說出口，但我一直都很感激您所做的一切。）

☺ 給父親 ☺

☆ Happy Father's Day! 　　　　　父親節快樂！

☆ Have a very happy Father's
　Day. 　　　　　　　　　　　　祝您有個快樂的父親節。

☆ You are the best dad in the
　world. 　　　　　　　　　　　您是世界上最好的爸爸。

☆ I am glad that you are my
　dad. 　　　　　　　　　　　　眞高興您是我爸爸。

☆ Have the best Father's Day
　ever. 　　　　　　　　　　　　祝您有個最棒的父親節。

☆ This is for all the things
that you have done for me.

這是為了感謝您為我所做的
一切。

☆ You are the best dad that a
kid ever had.

您是孩子心目中,最好的爸
爸。

☆ You have been there when I
needed you.

在我需要您的時候,您總是
在那裡。

☆ Father's Day is a time to
remember all the good things
that dads do for us.

父親節是憶起爸爸們為我們
所做的一切的時刻。

☆ I love you more than anything
else.

我愛您勝過一切。

☆ Thanks for helping me *through
the tough times*.

謝謝您幫我度過許多艱苦的
時光。

☆ How could I be so lucky to
have a dad like you.

我竟是如此幸運,能有像您
這樣的父親。

☆ All my love to the dearest
father in the world.

將我全部的愛,獻給我最親
愛的爸爸。

☆ *It is sometimes hard to say*,
but I am always grateful for
what you have done.

雖然有時很難說出口,但是
我一直都十分感激您所作的
一切。

☆ We all love you, dad.

我們全都愛您,爸。

---

tough〔tʌf〕 *adj.* 困難的;艱苦的

☆ You have always been so
patient with me.

您對我總是那麼地有耐性。

☆ To father — from your favorite string bean.

給父親——您最寵愛的小豆
子上。

☆ We combined efforts to make
this card for you. *It may not
be the greatest*, but it is
made with love.

我們同心協力，作成了這張
卡片。它也許不是最好的，
但它是用愛心製成的。

☆ You are a little different from
the rest of us, but that's OK.
You are still my dad.

您和我們有點不同，但是沒
有關係，您還是我爸爸。

☆ You are the best, dad.

爸爸，您是最好的。

☆ I will flatter you today.

今天我要好好對您獻殷勤。

☆ I think of you often.

我時常想念您。

☆ So sorry that I can't be
there for Father's Day.

很抱歉，我沒辦法和您共度
父親節。

☆ I wish that I was there
with you.

但願我能陪您過節。

☆ No distance is too great that
love cannot connect.

千山萬水，阻隔不了我對您
的敬愛。

***

combine〔kəm'baɪn〕*v.* 結合
flatter〔'flætɚ〕*v.* 巴結；獻殷勤

☆ Over the years *we have had our differences*, but I always love you.

這些年來，雖然我們常有意見不和的地方，但我一直敬愛著您。

☆ I look back on all of my years and consider myself lucky because I have you as my dad.

回顧我以往的所有歲月，我認為自己是幸運的，因為我擁有您這樣的父親。

☆ Thanks for holding my hand when I needed it.

謝謝您，在我需要協助的時候，伸出援手。

☆ I *owe* all of my skills of fatherhood *to* you Dad. Happy Father's Day.

爸爸，我所有的為父之道，都受恩於您。祝您父親節快樂。

☆ I didn't realize that being a father would be so difficult. It makes me appreciate you all the more.

我不知道，做一個父親，竟然會這麼困難。那使我更加感激您。

☆ Now that I am a father, I can see what a good job you did in raising us.

現在我已身為人父。我才知道，您在養育我們時，做得多麼好。

☆ I didn't see what a good father you were to us before, but I do now.

我不知道您以前是一個多麼好的父親，但是現在我知道了。

☆ Pa, without your strength and wisdom, *I would never be the person that I am today.*

爸，如果沒有您的力量和智慧，我不會成為今天的我。

☆ Your experience and guidance have always been appreciated.　您的經歷和引導，一直讓我衷心感激。

☺ 給祖父 ☺

☆ *Happy Father's Day*, granddad.　父親節快樂，爺爺。

☆ To my wonderful Grandfather on Father's Day.　在父親節這一天，送給我最好的祖父。

☆ A warm wish from your grandson on Father's Day.　你的孫兒，在父親節向您獻上溫馨的祝福。

☆ Grandpa, we love you. Happy Father's Day.　爺爺，我們愛您。父親節快樂。

☆ Here is a Father's Day greeting from your granddaughter.　孫女在此向您問候，父親節快樂。

☆ Your granddaughter sends you Father's Day wishes.　孫女向您致上父親節的祝福。

☆ If we didn't live so far apart, I would come to see you every day.　如果我們沒住得這麼遠，我會每天來看您。

☆ I may not be able to see you, but I can send you this card *with love*.　我也許無法來看您，但我可以送您這張愛的卡片。

☆ Give gramma a big hug for me too.　也替我擁抱一下奶奶。

☆ We all love you grampa. 　爺爺，我們都愛您。

☆ I will ask mom and dad when 　我會問問媽和爸，何時我們
we can come to see you. 　能來看您。

☆ I hope that you can come and 　我希望不久，您能來和我們
stay with us soon. 　住在一起。

☆ You deserve to be flattered 　今天您應該被奉承一番。
today.

☆ I think that you are the great- 　我認為，您是世上最偉大的
est grandfather *in the world*. 　祖父。

☆ Your experience and wisdom is 　我們需要及感激您的經驗與
needed and appreciated. 　智慧。

☆ There is a gift for you in the 　在信裡，有份送您的禮物。
mail.

☆ I hope you like the present I 　希望您喜歡我送給您的禮物。
sent you.

☆ I made a present for you. I 　我做了件禮物給您。希望您
hope you like it. 　會喜歡。

☆ I hope the sweater that I 　希望我為您打的那件毛衣很
made for you fits. 　合身。

---

sweater〔'swɛtɚ〕 *n.* 毛衣

Sample Cards for Father's Day

父親節卡片範例

爲您的賀卡添新粧

Dear Grandpa,

I know that I have been silent for a long time. I am sorry for not writing to you. But you are not far from my thoughts.

Your grandson, Adam

親愛的爺爺：

我知道我已經好久都沒有消息了。非常抱歉，沒有給您寫信。但我一直都惦記著您。

您的孫兒　亞當上

Dear Dad,

I may not see you often, but I think of you all the time. Happy Father's Day!

Your daughter, Marie

親愛的爸爸：

或許我不常看到您，但我總是想念著您。父親節快樂！

您的女兒　瑪麗亞上

Dear Dad,

Here is a Father's Day card and gift from afar. Although the distance between us is great, my love for you is as close as it ever was. I will see you and mom real soon. Take care and give my love to mom too.

Your son,
Kelly

親愛的爸爸:

　　這是從遠方寄來的父親節卡片和禮物。雖然我們彼此相隔遙遠,我對您的愛却和從前一樣親近。我會儘快回來與您和媽媽相聚。請多保重,並轉達我的愛給媽。

您的兒子
凱利上

** distance〔'dɪstəns〕 *n.* 距離

Unit 7 ——— *For-Teacher's-Day* ———
教師節

《 **To Sir with love** 》

　　中國人一向是最尊師重道的民族。每年的**教師節**（ *Teach-er's Day* ）也正是學生們向老師，表達謝意與敬意的日子。連平常最淘氣的學生，也不忘在老師的桌上，放一張小卡片，上面寫著：" *I promise not to put a frog in Ketty's bag any more!* "（ 我答應您，再也不將青蛙放到凱蒂的袋子裡了! ）

😊 一般祝賀語 😊

☆ Thank you, teacher.　　　　　謝謝您，老師。

☆ We all want to thank you.　　我們全體要向您致謝。

☆ Here is a big thank you from　這是我們全體對您的感謝之
all of us to you.　　　　　　意。

☆ We can't thank you enough.　我們對您感激不盡。

☆ *From the bottom of* our hearts　我們打從心底，深深地感激
we give you a big thank you.　你。

☆ No one else deserves a bigger　沒有人比您，值得更深切的
thank you than you.　　　　感謝。

☆ We are grateful to you.　　　我們感激您。

☆ I am truly grateful to you, teacher.　　　老師，我眞的萬分感激您。

☆ My grateful sentiments come from the heart.　　　我滿懷感恩之情。

☆ We are grateful for all that you have done.　　　你爲我們所做的事，我們都很感激。

☆ It is hard to express our gratefulness.　　　我們很難表達我們的謝意。

☆ This card is only a small token of our gratefulness.　　　這張卡片只代表了我們的感激之心。

☆ On this day *we honor you*.　　　在這個日子，我們向您致敬。

☆ It is the appropriate time for showing you our thanks.　　　現在正是我們表露對您感激的最佳時機。

☆ This day is especially for you.　　　這一天是特別爲您慶祝的。

☆ This special day is for us to say thank you.　　　這是讓我們向您說聲「謝謝」的特別日子。

☆ It is appropriate that we should have a special day for you.　　　給您一個特別的日子，這是應該的。

☆ One day is hardly enough to show our thankfulness.　　　以一天來表示我們的感激，是不夠的。

**——————————————

grateful〔'gretfəl〕*adj*. 感激的　　token〔'tokən〕*n*. 象徵
appropriate〔ə'proprɪ,et〕*adj*. 適合的

☆ This is Confucius' birthday and a time to be grateful to all teachers.

今天是孔子誕辰，也是向所有老師致謝的日子。

☆ Confucius' birthday is the right day to be grateful to you.

孔子誕辰紀念日，正是向您致謝的日子。

☆ With every year's passing, we honor Confucius and you.

每一年，我們都向孔子與您致敬。

☆ There is no better opportunity to honor you, than on Confucius' birthday.

沒有比孔子誕辰更好的時機，來向你致敬了。

☆ You are an important part of the Chinese tradition of teachers—just like Confucius.

您是中國教師傳統中，重要的一部分——就如孔子一般。

☆ The Confucian tradition lives on through you.

在您身上，可以看到儒家傳統精神的延續。

☆ I wish to express my gratefulness to you for instructing my child.

感謝您辛苦地教導我的小孩。

☆ My child *speaks highly of you*. Thank you.

我的孩子很推崇您。謝謝您。

＊＊————————————————

opportunity〔͵ɑpəˈtjunətɪ〕*n*. 機會；時機
Confucian tradition 儒家傳統

☆ Thank you for being my child's teacher.

謝謝您作爲我孩子的老師。

☆ Everyone should be grateful for teachers. Thank you for teaching my children.

每個人都應感謝老師。謝謝您教導我的孩子們。

☆ As parents we recognize the value of you in our child's development. Thank you for what you have done.

身爲父母，我們體認到，您在我們孩子發展過程中的重要性。謝謝您所做的一切。

☆ No one is more grateful than us.

沒有人比我們更感激您。

☆ We may not be the best students, but we are always grateful.

我們也許不是最好的學生，但我們一直心存感激。

☆ I may not always be a *model student*, but I do thank you for all that you have done.

我也許不是個模範生，但我眞的感謝您所做的一切。

☆ Our class gets a little *out of hand* at times, but we do respect you.

我們班有時有點難以管教，但我們眞的敬愛您。

☆ I hope to *earn your respect* someday.

盼望有天您能對我刮目相看。

☆ You have my eternal respect.

我永遠敬愛您。

---

recognize〔'rεkəg,naɪz〕v. 認定　　*model student* 模範生
respect〔rɪ'spεkt〕n. 尊敬

☆ I sometimes don't like school, but I am always grateful for your efforts.

有時我不喜歡學校，但我一直感激您所作的努力。

☆ Here is a small token of my appreciation.

這是我感激之心小小的象徵。

☆ This apple is for you. Thank you teacher.

這顆蘋果送給您。謝謝您，老師。

☆ My mother says that we should thank the teacher today. Thank you teacher.

我媽說，今天我們應該謝謝老師。謝謝您，老師。

☆ We all *pitched in* to buy you this gift. We are grateful to you, teacher.

這是我們大夥湊錢買給您的禮物。我們很感激您，老師。

☆ No one deserves this present more than you. Thank you teacher.

沒有人比您更應得這份禮物。謝謝您，老師。

☆ This gift comes from the heart.

這份禮是真心送給您的。

☆ I promise that I will do better in school.

我保證以後在學校一定表現得很好。

☆ You know that I try. But I know that I need to try harder.

你知道我試著做到。但我知道我還需要更努力。

** —

pitch in 參加；貢獻

☆ Thank you for your kind words to me. *Happy Teacher's Day*.

謝謝您慈藹的教誨。祝您教師節快樂。

☆ You have been a great teacher and an even better friend. Thank you for all that you have done.

你一直是個好老師，甚至是位更好的朋友。謝謝您所做的一切。

☆ You have made me want to become a teacher. I am grateful to you.

你已經使我想為人師表了。我很感激您。

☆ I send to you everlasting feelings of gratefulness and thankfulness.

謹致上永恆的謝意與感激。

＊＊────────────────

everlasting〔,ɛvɚˈlæstɪŋ〕*adj.* 永恆的

Sample Cards for Teacher's Day

教師節卡片範例　　　爲您的賀卡添新粧

Dear Sir,

　　You are like a third parent.
We all love you.

　　　　　　　Class 102

親愛的老師：

　　您就像是我們的大家長。我們都愛您。

　　　　　　　　　　102班

To Sir with love,

　　We all like having you as our teacher,
although we don't always behave well
in class.

　　　　From all of us

給摯愛的老師：

　　雖然我們有時不乖，但是我們仍然喜歡您當我們的老師。

　　　　　　　我們全體同學　上

** **behave well** 行爲合宜

Dear Miss Wang,

　We wish to show our gratitude
and thankfulness with a small gift.
Have a happy Teacher's Day!

　　　　David and Joe

親愛的王小姐：

　　我們要送您一份小禮，表示我們對您的感激之意。教師節愉快！

　　　　　　　　　　大衛和喬

** gratitude〔'grætəˌtjud〕*n.* 感激

Dear Miss Chen,

　I don't finish my assignments
on time sometimes, but you have
my respect and gratefulness.

　　　　　Tom

親愛的陳小姐：

　　雖然有時候，我沒能準時交作業，但我還是尊敬您，感謝您。

　　　　　　　　　　湯姆

** assignment〔ə'saɪnmənt〕*n.* 作業

Dear Miss Lee,

This is Confucious' birthday and a time to be grateful to all teachers. It is a profession that deserves such special recognition. There is no more appropriate time than this to honor you and others in your chosen field. You have my eternal gratefulness.

Your student,
Matthew

親愛的李小姐:

今天是孔子誕辰,也是向所有教師致謝的日子。這個職業值得特別受到如此地重視與肯定。現在是向您及在您所選擇的行業中,其他的人致敬的最佳時機。我永遠感激您。

您的學生　馬休上

** profession〔prə'fɛʃən〕n. 職業
recognition〔͵rɛkəg'nɪʃən〕n. 肯定
eternal〔ɪ'tɝnḷ〕adj. 永恆的

Unit 8 — For Thanksgiving —

感恩節

≪ **Praise God!** ≫

　　最早的美國移民，在經過拓荒的長久辛苦之後，終於有了大豐收，爲了感念上帝的恩德，而開始有**感恩節**（*Thanksgiving*）。定每年十一月的第四個星期四爲感恩節。這一天，全家人都會團聚在一起，享用準備好的火雞（*turkey*）、南瓜派等大餐。對於當天無法回來的人，就會寄張祝福卡給他。

一般祝福語

☆ Happy Thanksgiving .　　　　　　感恩節快樂。

☆ Wishing you and yours a happy　　祝福你們全家感恩節快樂。
　Thanksgiving.

☆ Warm wishes at Thanksgiving.　　在感恩節，衷心地祝福你們。

☆ From all of us to all of you　　　我們全體祝你們感恩節快樂。
　at Thanksgiving.

☆ Have a joyous and happy　　　　　祝你們有一個歡樂愉快的感
　Thanksgiving.　　　　　　　　　　恩節。

** joyous〔'dʒɔɪəs〕*adj.* 快樂的

☆ *Thanksgiving wishes* for you
and your family.

給你們全家感恩節的祝福。

☆ I wish you could be here on
Thanksgiving.

但願你能來過感恩節。

☆ Thanksgiving just won't be
the same without you.

沒有你，感恩節就不會一樣
了。

☆ This will be our first Thanksgiving apart.

這將是我們第一次不在一起
過感恩節。

☆ The table will seem empty
without you.

沒有你，感恩節的餐桌會顯
得空蕩蕩。

☆ It will be sad not to see you
during the holiday when fam-
ilies *get together.*

家人團聚的節日裡，不能看
到你，我會感到難過。

☆ This is to our first Thanksgiving together.

致我們第一次的感恩節相聚。

☆ Our first Thanksgiving will
be the most memorable.

我們第一次共度的感恩節，
將最值得懷念。

☆ Here's to many more Thanksgivings to come.

致未來無數個感恩節。

＊＊ ────────────────

empty〔'ɛmptɪ〕*adj.* 空的；空虛的
memorable〔'mɛmərəbļ〕*adj.* 值得紀念的

☆ Our first Thanksgiving should
be our best.

我們第一次共度的感恩節，
是我們最美好的時光。

☆ It may not seem like much,
but it is our first Thanksgiving together.

也許看起來不太像，但這可
是我們第一次共度感恩節囉。

☆ I wouldn't want to spend
Thanksgiving with anyone else.

我只願和你共度感恩節。

☆ This is the first *in a long
line* of Thanksgivings to come.

這是未來無數感恩節的第一
個。

☆ To so many more happy
Thanksgivings together.

致往後共度的無數個快樂感
恩節。

☆ What a wonderful time to be
together.

在一起的時光多麼快樂。

☆ Thanksgiving is a time when
I tell you that I love you.

感恩節就是我告訴你，我愛
你的時候。

☆ The first Thanksgiving seems
the most awkward, *but filled
with love*.

第一次的感恩節似乎最糟糕，
但卻充滿了愛。

☆ To my lovely parents at
Thanksgiving.

在此感恩節，祝福我可愛的
父母。

＊＊

---

wonderful 〔'wʌndəfəl〕 *adj.* 奇妙的；極好的
awkward 〔'ɔkwəd〕 *adj.* 笨拙的；糟糕的

☆ Happy Thanksgiving to *a couple of* wonderful kids.

祝我這些可愛的孩子們，感恩節快樂。

☆ Thanksgiving is a great time to tell you that we love you kids.

孩子，感恩節這時刻，我們要說：我們都愛你們。

☆ Your grandson wishes you a wonderful Thanksgiving.

你的孫兒祝福你們有一個美好的感恩節。

☆ Here is a Thanksgiving card to my favorite aunt and uncle.

致上感恩節卡片一張，給我最親愛的叔叔嬸嬸！

☆ Thanksgiving is the best holiday of the year.

感恩節是一年中最好的節日。

☆ I love to eat, so I love Thanksgiving.

我愛吃，所以我喜歡感恩節。

☆ I hope you are feeling thankful after your supper.

希望你吃過晚飯後，有感恩的心情。

☆ Thanksgiving is a time to *think of* your family and friends.

感恩節是我們想到家人和朋友的時刻。

☆ *At Thanksgiving* we should think of the less fortunate.

在感恩節時，我們要想到那些不幸的人們。

** ───────────────

thankful〔'θæŋkfəl〕*adj*. 感謝的；感激的　　supper〔'sʌpɚ〕*n*. 晚餐
fortunate〔'fɔrtʃənɪt〕*adj*. 幸運的

☆ Let us observe a moment of silence for those who are not able to be so thankful.

讓我們爲那些無法心存感激的人們靜默片刻。

☆ Thanksgiving is a time to seriously consider our place in this world and *be thankful for* what the good Lord has given us.

感恩節是我們認眞地考慮，我們在這世上所處的地位，感謝上蒼所有賜予的時刻。

☆ To give thanks at Thanksgiving we should help the less fortunate.

在感恩節表達感謝，我們應該幫助那些不幸的人。

☆ We all have something to be thankful for.

我們多少有要感謝別人之處。

☆ *I have you to be thankful for.*

我感謝你。

☆ We should be thankful for our loved ones, friends and everything in the world.

我們應該感謝我們所愛的人，朋友和世界上每一件事物。

☆ Let's think about all the things we have to be thankful for.

讓我們想想所有該感謝的人或事。

**

observe〔əb'zɝv〕v. 保持　　silence〔'saɪləns〕n. 寂靜；緘默
seriously〔'sɪrɪəslɪ〕adv. 嚴肅地；認眞地
consider〔kən'sɪdə〕v. 考慮；思考

☆ Save the dark meat for me.　　　　爲我留份雞腿。

☆ I am getting hungry just　　　　一想到它我就餓了。
thinking about it.

☆ I love Thanksgiving: Friends,　　我喜歡感恩節：因爲有朋友，
food, and football.　　　　　　食物和足球賽。

☆ I will be home for Thanks-　　　我會回家過感恩節，所以要
giving so save a little turkey　　留點火雞給我。
for me.

☆ There are only 31 more shop-　　離聖誕還有三十一個採購日。
ping days until Christmas.

** ────────────────

dark meat 黑肉（ 雞腿等肉色較深的部位 ）
turkey 〔'tɝkɪ 〕 n. 火雞

Sample Cards for Thanksgiving

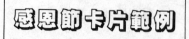

感恩節卡片範例

爲您的賀卡添新粧
....

Dear Maggie,
    The things that we share on
Thanksgiving will carry me forever.

                Philip

親愛的瑪姬：

    在感恩節裡，我們擁有的點點滴滴，令我永難忘懷。

                菲力普上

** share〔ʃɛr〕*v.* 分享

Daddy and Mommy,
    We would like to take this
opportunity to say：We love you.

          Your sons

爹地和媽咪：

    藉此機會，我們要說：我們愛您。

              你們的兒子　敬上

** opportunity〔ˌɑpəˈtjunətɪ〕*n.* 機會

Dear Mom and Dad,

I can't wait for Thanksgiving.
There is all the food that I really
like. I also love to see all of you.
And lastly, I love to relax and
watch the games on TV. I will be
home for Thanksgiving, so save
some delicious dishes for me.

Your son,
Andy

親愛的爸媽：

我等不及要過感恩節了。有所有我
喜歡的食物。我更喜歡見到你們。最後，
我喜歡放鬆自己，看看電視。我會回家
過感恩節，所以要留些可口的菜給我。

你們的兒子

安迪 上

** lastly〔ˈlæstlɪ；ˈlɑstlɪ〕adv. 最後地；最後一點
relax〔rəˈlæks；rɪˈlæks〕v. 放鬆；鬆弛

● 心得筆記欄 ●

Chapter 3

有情天地篇

Unit 1 ——*Wedding-Cards*——
結婚賀卡

≪ **Best wishes always !** ≫

　　結婚（*marriage*）是個接受祝福，分享喜悅的時刻。如果你能為新人挑選一張精緻的賀卡，並附上親筆書寫的祝福，那麼，將更能表達你的誠摯心意。若你想送份賀禮，則可寫上：
"*Your wedding gift is on its way. I hope you like it.*"
（你的結婚賀禮，正在寄送當中。希望你會喜歡。）

😃 給兒女 😃

☆ Your father and I wish you
well. We love your new wife
and our new daughter.

你父親和我都祝福你。我們愛你的新婚妻子，也就是我們的新女兒。

☆ She is a beautiful addition
to the family.

這個家庭，增添了一位美麗的成員。

☆ You couldn't have ***asked for***
a better husband.

你再也找不到，這麼好的丈夫。

☆ He will make a fine son- in-
law and great father.

他將是一位好女婿及好爸爸。

**————————————————

addition〔ə'dɪʃən〕*n*. 增加物

☆ If either of you need any advice, just ask. Your mother and I have a little experience in marriage.

如果你們其中有人想聽些建議，儘管問吧。你媽和我，對於婚姻都是過來人。

☆ She is a fine woman and the most beautiful **daughter-in-law** I could have asked for.

她是個賢淑的女人，而且是我所能選到的，最漂亮的媳婦。

☆ Here is a small gift from your mother and I to help you get started.

這是你媽和我，所送的一份小禮，希望能幫助你早日安頓下來。

☆ Love and wishes to you and our new **son-in-law** on this wedding day.

在你們的大喜之日，給妳和我們的女婿，所有的愛和祝福。

☆ I know that he will make a fine father.

我知道他會是一個好爸爸。

☆ It is hard for me to believe that my baby girl is getting married.

實在很難相信，自己的小女孩要出嫁了。

☆ Your happy married life is our great hope.

你們的婚姻幸福，是我們最大的心願。

☆ My lovely child, remember one thing : Love what you choose; and choose what you love !

我可愛的孩子,記住一件事:愛你所選擇；選擇你所愛！

🔟 給親戚 🔟

☆ I never thought that my kid sister would get married. Congratulations！

我從來沒想過，我的小妹會出嫁。恭喜妳！

☆ He will make a fine brother-in-law. Congratulations.

他會是一個好妹夫的。恭喜。

☆ She will be a great wife and an even better sister-in-law.

她不但會是一個賢妻，而且更會是一個好嫂子。

☆ A wish from your brothers and sisters on your wedding day.

你的兄弟姐妹，祝你新婚快樂。

☆ We wish you every happiness that comes from *lasting love* and all those things you are dreaming of.

願你堅彌的愛情，和所有夢寐以求的事物，能爲你帶來快樂與幸福。

☆ We wish you *true contentment*, a life that's filled with sharing, and most of all, we wish you joy that comes from deeply caring.

我們願你能得到眞正的幸福與滿足，並擁有相互犧牲，奉獻的一生，更重要的是，願你能從彼此深切的關注中，得到喜悅。

＊＊────────────

brother-in-law〔'brʌðɚɪn,lɔ〕 *n.* 姊夫；妹夫
dream〔drim〕 *v.* 做夢   contentment〔kən'tɛntmənt〕 *n.* 滿足

☆ Best wishes always. Keep
  in touch, sis.

祝妳永遠幸福。保持聯繫，
姐姐。

☆ Best wishes for the future,
  Uncle John.

祝您未來順心如意，約翰叔
叔。

☆ Well sister, I am truly happy for you on your wedding
  day. Have a wonderful and
  romantic honeymoon.

嗯，姐姐，妳要結婚了，我
眞替妳感到高興。願妳擁有
一個既奇妙又浪漫的蜜月。

☆ It is hard to believe that
  I now have a sister-in-law.
  Congratulations, and may
  happiness be with you.

很難相信現在自己有了個妹
夫。恭喜妳，願幸福常伴著
妳。

☆ I hope you know what you
  are doing. But good luck
  anyway.

但願你知道你在做甚麼。不
過無論如何，祝你好運。

☆ Please convey my congratulations to your Ted.

請把我的祝賀之意，轉達給
妳的泰德。

☆ *Please accept my best wishes*
  for the two of you.

請接受我對你們衷心的祝福。

✱✱──────────────

romantic〔roˊmæntɪk〕*adj.* 浪漫的
convey〔kənˊve〕*v.* 傳達

☺ 給朋友 ☺

☆ I hope that this is the beginning of a wonderful life
together.

我希望這是你們美好生活的
開始。

☆ I wish you much happiness
together.

願你倆婚姻幸福美滿。

☆ Best wishes for many years
of happiness for the two of
you.

願你倆百年好合。

☆ Best wishes for a joyful
home together.

願你倆組織一個快樂的二人
世界。

☆ May everyday in your life
together be as full of happiness and joy as your wedding day.

願你倆的每一天，都能像新
婚時一樣，洋溢着快樂和喜
悅。

☆ The two of you make *a
perfect couple*.

你們倆眞是天造地設的一對。

☆ You certainly have found
yourself a wonderful wife.

毫無疑問地，你已爲自己找
到一位好妻子了。

☆ I am sure that he will
make a wonderful husband.

我相信他一定會是個好丈夫。

**───────────────

joyful〔ˈdʒɔɪfəl〕*adj.* 愉快的　　perfect〔ˈpɝfɪkt〕*adj.* 完美的
couple〔ˈkʌpḷ〕*n.* 夫婦　　certainly〔ˈsɝtṇlɪ〕*adv.* 毫無疑問地

☆ ***For a special couple*** : Congratulations on your wedding.

獻給一對與眾不同的新人：祝新婚快樂。

☆ A wish from all of us on your wedding day.

在你的大喜之日，致上我們全體的祝福。

☆ I know you both well and feel that your marriage will last for a long time.

我很了解你們，覺得你們的婚姻定可天長地久。

☆ Congratulations and good luck, kids.

孩子們，恭喜你們，並祝你們鴻運高照。

☆ I am filled with such joy ***at the sight of*** you two beginning together.

看見你倆開始生活在一起，我內心充滿了歡愉。

☆ Seeing you two ***reminds*** me ***of*** my wedding day.

你們讓我想起了我結婚的時候。

☆ Wedding bells are breaking up that gang of mine.

結婚的鐘聲響起，拆散了我昔日的那一群伙伴。

☆ This one is going to last. I just know it.

我知道，你們定能白頭偕老，百年好合。

☆ You couldn't have picked a better girl.

你再也找不到這麼好的女孩了。

＊＊ ─────────────────

congratulation〔kən͵grætʃə'leʃən〕*n.* 祝賀；慶賀

last〔læst〕*v.* 持續；維持　　remind〔rɪ'maɪnd〕*v.* 提醒；喚起

gang〔gæŋ〕*n.* 群；幫派

☆ I can't think of a nicer wife for you.

我想不出還有誰，更適合當你的妻子。

☆ This is truly a joyous time. Congratulations and good luck.

這真是快樂的一刻。恭喜你，祝你好運。

☆ We wish that you will be contented every year.

祝福你們歡樂年年。

☆ Marriage is a life of sharing.

婚姻就是分享生活的一切。

☆ Congratulations and have a beautiful honeymoon.

恭喜你們，祝你們有個美好的蜜月假期。

☆ You two are the prince and princess in a fairy tale and may you live happily ever-after !

你倆正如童話故事中的王子和公主，祝福你們永遠幸福快樂！

☆ May you two always be *in love* ! May happiness increase with age !

祝你倆永浴愛河,白頭偕老!

☆ May you two have a lovely baby !

祝你們早生貴子。

☆ I feel certain that you are just right for each other.

我相信你們是最適合的一對。

---

contented〔kən'tɛntɪd〕*adj.* 滿足的   honeymoon〔'hʌnɪ,mun〕*n.* 蜜月
fairy tale 童話故事

Sample Wedding Cards

結婚賀卡範例

把您的祝福包裝起來

Dear Henry,
　　Now I understand why
we've seen so little of you
recently! Congratulations!
　　　　　　　　Eric

親愛的亨利：
　　現在我知道，為什麼最近很少看到你了！恭喜你了！
　　　　　　　　艾利克

** recently〔ˊrisəntlı〕*adv*. 最近；近來

Dear Annie,
　　I can't think of two
people more suited to each
other than you and David.
　　　Your sister Eliza

親愛的安妮：
　　我再也想不出，有比你和大衛更相配的佳偶了。
　　　　　　　你的妹妹依莉莎　上

Dear Joanna,

Although I have'nt met Peter yet, I am sure if he is your choice he must be the best.

Frances

親愛的喬安娜：

雖然我尚未和彼得見過面，但是我確信，如果他是妳的選擇，那他必然是最好的。

法蘭西斯

Dear Scott,

On the occasion of your marriage, I wish you and Emily ever increasing happiness and the best of everything in the world.

Your Uncle Matthew

親愛的史考特：

在你新婚之際，祝你和艾茉莉永遠幸福快樂，享有世界上最美好的一切。

你的馬休叔叔

Dear Catherine,

I am delighted to receive the announcement of your marriage and now send you and your Frank my sincere congratulations and best wishes for a happy and harmonious life together !

Your brother,
Edward

親愛的凱瑟琳：

很高興收到妳的結婚通知，此時，向妳及妳的法蘭克，致上我誠摯的祝賀，祝福你們琴瑟和諧，婚姻美滿！

妳的哥哥
愛德華

** announcement〔əˋnaʊnsmənt〕*n*. 通知
sincere〔sɪnˋsɪr〕*adj*. 誠摯的；衷心的

My lovely Jennifer,

A wedding wish for you. "Together" is a lovely word——a word that time endears. It means a kind of sweetness that grows sweeter through the years. Sending you my blessing and congratulations again.

Teresa

我可愛的珍妮佛：

向妳致上婚禮的祝福。「在一起」是個可愛的字眼——一個因時間而更加親密的字眼。它代表著一種，隨著歲月的遞嬗而更加甜美的感覺。再次寄上我的祝福與祝賀！

泰莉莎

** endear〔ɪn'dɪr〕 *v.* 使親密；使喜愛

Engagement-Cards
訂婚賀卡

≪ **Congratulations !** ≫

訂婚（ *engagement* ）是爲以後的婚禮作準備。除了獻上對新人的祝福之外，在外國還流行一種稱爲 " *wedding shower* " 的聚會，就是在婚禮前夕，親朋好友紛紛將一些家庭用品送給新人，因爲禮物如雨般而來，故稱 *shower* 。

☻ 訂婚賀卡祝福語 ☻

☆ May you two always be in love.

願你倆永浴愛河 。

☆ Congratulations on your engagement.

恭喜你們訂婚 。

☆ We wish you success and happiness in your future marriage.

我們祝福你們，婚禮成功，生活幸福 。

☆ Good luck to you. *We think you make a fine couple*.

祝你們事事如意 。我們認爲你們是天生的一對 。

**

engagement〔 ɪnˈgedʒmənt 〕 *n.* 訂婚

☆ We are so happy for the both of you.

我們為你們兩人感到高興。

☆ I couldn't think of a nicer couple.

我想不出比你們更理想的一對。

☆ He is really the best one of the bunch.

他確實是我們這群中最好的。

☆ You found yourself a real catch.

你找到一個真正適合結婚的對象了。

☆ Engagements are a time of searching yourself, and discovering what it really means to love.

訂婚是個研究自己，並且發現什麼才值得去愛的時間。

☆ With an engagement you discover in yourself the true meaning of love.

訂婚後，你就會發現，什麼是愛的真諦。

☆ Engagement is the final stage of courtship. It is the most beautiful.

訂婚是戀愛的最後階段。它是最美麗的。

☆ She is going to be the most beautiful bride *in the world*.

她將會是世界上最美麗的新娘。

**

bunch 〔 bʌntʃ 〕 *n.* 群　　catch 〔 kætʃ 〕 *n.* 〔俗〕宜於結婚的對象
search 〔 sɝtʃ 〕 *v.* 研究　　courtship 〔 ˈkortʃɪp 〕 *n.* 戀愛

☆ What a wonderful couple you two make.

你們兩人，眞是佳偶天成。

☆ How wonderful the both of you are.

你們這一對璧人眞是太棒了。

☆ Engagement is the time to prepare for your future days.

訂婚是爲未來的日子做準備。

☆ To a fine grandson and his *new bride to be*.

給我的乖孫子和他未來的新娘。

☆ You are a beautiful grand-daughter. Your grandfather and I wish you success in your future marriage.

妳是位美麗的孫女。妳爺爺和我祝福妳婚姻美滿。

☆ He will make a fine grandson-in-law.

他會是一個很好的孫女婿。

☆ I know that you will make my granddaughter happy.

我知道，你會讓我的孫女兒快樂。

☆ My grandson has told me that he is the happiest man in the world. Thank you and good luck.

我孫子告訴我，他是世界上最快樂的人。謝謝妳，祝妳事事如意。

☆ Joe, I think that she will make a great wife.

喬，我想她會是一個很好的妻子。

**——————————————

bride 〔 braɪd 〕 *n.* 新娘

☆ *I am overjoyed with* the thought of your wedding.

一想到你的婚禮，我就非常高興。

☆ I can't wait to meet my new sister-in-law to be.

我等不及要見我的新嫂嫂。

☆ Well, *it is about time* that you asked her for her hand.

嗯，也該是你向她求婚的時候了。

☆ With this card I do wish you a wonderful marriage. Good luck！

謹以這張卡片，我祝福你們有個美滿的姻緣。祝你們萬事如意！

＊＊

　　overjoyed〔ˈovɚˈdʒɔɪd〕*adj.* 極高興的

Sample Engagement Cards

訂婚賀卡範例

把您的祝福包裝起來

Dear Jessica and Charlie,
　　We can't think of a better choice
for a spouse. We will see you at the
wedding!
　　　　　　Stella and Louis

親愛的潔西嘉和查理：

　　我們想不出，比你們更好的佳偶了。婚禮上見！

　　　　　　史黛拉和路易　上

** spouse〔spauz〕*n.* 配偶　　wedding〔ˈwɛdɪŋ〕*n.* 婚禮

Dad,
　　I like Carol very much, and I
know that she makes you very happy.
You have my full support on this wedding.
　　　　　　Your daughter
　　　　　　Jenny

爹地：

　　我很喜歡凱若爾，我知道你們在一起很快樂。我完全支持你們。

　　　　　　你的女兒珍妮　上

** support〔səˈport〕*n.* 支持

Dear Shirley,

It is hard to believe that my little girl has grown up. I am so happy for you and your new husband to be.

Uncle Joe

親愛的雪莉：

真難相信，我的小女孩已經長大了。我為妳和未來的夫婿感到高興。

喬叔叔　上

** *grow up* 長大

My lovely daughter,

I want you to wear the wedding dress that I wore when I was married. Congratulations and good luck.

Your Mommy

我可愛的女兒：

我希望妳也穿上我結婚時，所穿的結婚禮服。恭喜妳，也祝妳好運。

妳的媽咪　上

** *wedding dress* 結婚禮服

Dear Mike,

I was so happy when I heard of your engagement to Nancy. You two have been going out for so long. It seems only fitting that you two get married. She will be a fine sister-in-law. Let me know when the wedding bells will be ringing.

Peggy

親愛的麥可：

我很高興聽到你和南茜訂婚的消息。你們已經約會這麼久了。似乎你們兩人只有結婚才合適。她會是一個好嫂嫂。當婚禮鐘聲要響起時，讓我知道。

佩姬上

** fitting〔'fɪtɪŋ〕*adj.* 合適的

bell〔bɛl〕*n.* 鐘

Unit  ──*Birthday-Cards*──

生日賀卡

≪ Happy Birthday！≫

每個人都有寄**生日卡**（ *birthday card* ）的經驗，但除了
Happy Birthday 之外，還可寫些什麼呢？如果是祝賀長輩的
生日，你可寫：" *Birthday greetings to you and many
happy returns of the day.* "（祝您福如東海，壽比南山。）
若是晚寄的生日卡，則可寫：" *I am sorry to be late in
sending you this card.* "（很抱歉延遲了你的生日卡。）

☺ 一般祝賀語 ☺

☆ Happy birthday to a marvelous
son.

給一個了不起的兒子，生日
快樂。

☆ Birthday greetings to the *apple of my eye*.

給我的寶貝，生日快樂。

☆ You are one year older today!

你今天老了一歲！

☆ Now you are getting bigger.
You are twenty years old.

現在你可長大些了。你二十
歲了。

---

marvelous〔'mɑrvḷəs〕*adj.* 了不起的
apple of sb's eye 某人珍愛之人

☆ *Happy birthday* from a bunch of clowns.

一群小丑祝你生日快樂。

☆ Smile, it is your birthday! It couldn't have happened to a nicer guy.

笑一下，這是你的生日。再也沒有人比你更好了。

☆ I am really luck to have a friend like you.

有一個像你這樣的朋友，我真是幸運。

☆ Wish you many more to come.

祝你要什麼有什麼。

☆ I am sorry to be late in sending this card.

很抱歉，我遲送了這張卡片。

☆ I hope you like the present that I am sending.

希望你喜歡我送你的禮物。

☆ Sincerest congratulations on your birthday.

真誠地祝福你生日快樂。

☆ *Way to go!* You made it through another year.

真要得！你又過了一年。

☺ 給朋友 ☺

☆ Birthdays are a time to *sit back* and reflect upon how much older you are.

生日就是輕鬆地坐下來，想一想自己又老多少的時間。

---

bunch〔bʌntʃ〕*n.* 群　　clown〔klaʊn〕*n.* 小丑

☆ You may be older, but are you any wiser?

你也許更老了，但你更聰明了嗎？

☆ You should feel lucky. Dogs age seven years every time we age one.

你應該覺得幸運。我們老一歲，狗可是老七歲呢。（狗的平均壽命只有人的七分之一。）

☆ I got you this card to *remind* you *of* your birthday. Happy Birthday.

我買這張卡片，是要提醒你，你的生日到了。生日快樂。

☆ You are 21. That is something to be proud of.

你二十一歲了。這真是值得驕傲的一件事。

☆ Let me ask you this: Would you like to be a kid again?

我來問你一個問題：你願意再當小孩嗎？

☆ Why don't we get together after work for a little party?

為什麼我們下班後，不聚一下，開個小派對呢？

☆ Happy Birthday. We are all taking you out for dinner and drinks. And you don't even have to *pay for* it.

生日快樂。我們大家要帶你出去吃晚餐，並且喝一杯。你甚至不用付錢呢。

☆ Just think how wise you are now.

只要想想看，你現在有多聰明。

---

remind〔rɪ'maɪnd〕*v.* 提醒　　kid〔kɪd〕*n.* 小孩

☆ We are going out and ***there is no getting out of it***. How else are we going to spend your birthday money?

我們要出去狂歡，沒有人可以缺席。還有什麼方法，可以讓我們花光你的錢呢？

☆ We all think that you are the greatest.

我們一直認為你是最棒的。

☺ 情侶之間 ☺

☆ Happy birthday, sweetheart.

甜心，生日快樂。

☆ I don't care how old you are. You are still ***tops with me***.

我不在乎你多大了。你對我而言，仍然是最好的。

☆ You deserve something special on your birthday, honey.

蜜糖，你生日時，應該得到一些特別的東西。

☆ For your birthday I will attempt to say "I love you" in 20 different ways.

我將試著，用二十種不同的方式對你說「我愛你」，做為你的生日禮物。

☆ We may grow old together, but ***as long as*** we are together I feel young.

我們也許會一起老去，但只要我們在一起，我就覺得年輕。

☆ You are sixteen going on seventeen

你現在是 16 歲，以後就是17歲了。

----

get out of 放棄   tops〔tɑps〕*adj*.〔俚〕最好的
deserve〔dɪˈzɝv〕*v*. 應得   attempt〔əˈtɛmpt〕*v*. 嘗試

☆ Like everyday, I am thinking of you with love on your birthday.

像每一天，我在你的生日，帶著愛意，想念著你。

☆ I want to wish you love and happiness on your birthday.

我願祝福你的生日，充滿愛和快樂。

☆ I have come to remind you that you are one year older now.

我要提醒你，你現在又長大一歲了。

☆ *Right now* I will give you this card for your birthday present.

現在我給你這張卡片，當做你的生日禮物。

☆ This card is good for one free kiss.

這張卡片值得妳以香吻來回報。

☆ Later tonight I will give you your real birthday present.

待會，今晚，我將給你一份眞正的生日禮物。

☆ *I am thinking of you as always.*

我會一直想念著你。

☆ I really want to be together on your birthday. I am sorry that we cannot.

在你的生日，我眞的想跟你共度。但是很抱歉，我們無法在一起。

😊 給父母親 😊

☆ *Happy birthday*, mom.

生日快樂，媽。

**

---

birthday present 生日禮物

☆ I hope you have a very happy
　birthday, dad.

願您有一個很愉快的生日，
爹地。

☆ Happy birthday to the best
　mom a son ever had.

祝兒子心目中最好的媽媽，
生日快樂。

☆ Wishing you happiness on your
　birthday, dad.

爸爸，祝您生日快樂。

☆ Mom and I want to take you
　out to your favorite restaurant.

媽和我要帶您到您最喜歡的
餐廳吃飯。

☆ Dad and I are going to treat
　you like a queen today.

爹地和我，今天要像侍候女
王般地侍候您。

☆ ***Have a wonderful day.***（Too
　bad you have to go to work.）

祝您整天都愉快。（可惜您
必須去工作。）

☆ Yet another year. That means
　I'm older, too.

又過了一年。那表示我也老
了一歲。

☆ Happy birthday Dad. You do
　not look a guy over 25. Were
　you bald at 25?

生日快樂，爸爸。您看起來
不像超過二十五歲。您二十
五歲就禿頭了嗎？

☆ I wish I could be there for
　your birthday. There is a
　little gift ***in the mail***.

可惜您生日時，我不能回去。
已經寄上一份小禮物。

** ────────────────────

favorite〔'fevərɪt〕*adj.* 最喜歡的
bald〔bɔld〕*adj.* 禿頭的

queen〔kwin〕*n.* 女王；皇后

☆ I am sorry that I can't be
there to celebrate with you.
I send my love and good wishes.

很抱歉，我無法伴隨您一起
慶祝生日。獻上我的愛以及
祝福。

☆ *On this birthday* I send all
my love to you. Happy Birthday to you.

在您的生日，我獻上所有的
愛。祝您生日快樂。

😊 給師長・上司 😊

☆ May the joy and peace of your
birthday always be with you.

願生日的快樂和平安，永遠
陪伴著您。

☆ Wishing you joy on your
birthday.

祝福您生日快樂。

☆ Birthday wishes *with special
thoughts.*

致上特別關切的生日祝福。

☆ May your birthday and every
other day be filled with happiness.

願您的生日和每一天，都充
滿了快樂。

☆ I hope your birthday brings
you much happiness.

願您的生日，帶給您更多的
快樂。

☆ I wish we could be together
on your birthday.

但願在您的生日，我們能夠
相聚。

---

celebrate〔ˋsɛləˏbret〕*v.* 慶祝

☆ Sincerest congratulations on your birthday.

最眞誠地祝賀您生日快樂。

☆ Birthday greetings to you and many *happy returns of the day.*

祝福您福如東海，壽比南山。

☆ Wishing you congratulations and *good health* on your birthday.

恭祝您生日快樂，身體健康。

☆ Wishing you birthday happiness.

祝您生日快樂。

☆ Sorry for forgetting your birthday. I usually try to forget my own.

很抱歉忘了您的生日。我本來一直試著要忘記自己的。

☺ 夫妻之間 ☺

☆ All my love and happiness on your birthday, dear.

親愛的，獻上我所有的愛和快樂，祝你生日快樂。

☆ Love and best wishes for your birthday.

以愛和最深切的祝福，祝你生日快樂。

☆ Happy birthday to the best wife in the world.

給全世界最好的妻子，生日快樂。

☆ I love you dearly. Happy birthday to you.

我眞誠地愛你。祝你生日快樂。

---

congratulation〔kən͵grætʃəˈleʃən〕*n.* 恭喜；祝賀
dearly〔ˈdɪrlɪ〕*adv.* 眞誠地；親愛地

☆ *To my loving husband*：Happy birthday.

給我親愛的丈夫：生日快樂。

☆ Here is a little something from me to you.　Happy birthday, dear.

這是我送你的一件小禮物。生日快樂，親愛的。

☆ I am really lucky to have a wife like you.

我實在很幸福，有像妳這樣好的妻子。

☆ You are the one that brings me so much happiness.　Happy birthday.

你帶給我這麼多的快樂。生日快樂。

☆ *Thinking of you*, dear, with endless love and affection on your birthday.

想念你，親愛的，以無限的愛和眞情，祝你生日快樂。

☆ I hope we can spend just as many as more years together.

希望我們能天長地久，永遠廝守在一起。

☆ Wishing you happiness always. Your loving husband.

祝妳永遠快樂。妳親愛的丈夫。

☆ Don't feel bad about growing old.　I am right behind you.

變老了,不要難過。我就在你後面。(比你年輕一點而已。)

**　—————————————**

affection〔əˈfɛkʃən〕*n.* 感情；眞情

Sample Birthday Cards

生日卡片範例

把您的祝福包裝起來

Dear Mary,
　　Watching you grow older only
reminds me that I am growing
older, too.
　　　　　　　　Julia

親愛的瑪麗：
　　看到妳又老了一歲，令我想到我也變老了。
　　　　　　　　茱莉亞

Dear Joe,
　　Happy birthday, big brother.
I hope today treats you well.
　　　　　　　　Angela

親愛的喬：
　　大哥哥，生日快樂。希望你今天過得很愉快。
　　　　　　　　安琪拉上

＊＊ treat〔trit〕*v.* 招待；款待

> *Big Mouth,*
>
> *To afford this birthday gift for you, I gave up expensive lunches and decided to brown-bag it for a week.*
>
> *Big Frog Frank*

大嘴巴：

　　為了要給你買生日禮物，我放棄了昂貴的午餐，而且決定這個星期都從家裡帶食物來當午餐。

大青蛙　法蘭克上

** afford〔əˋfɔrd〕v. 有足夠的（金錢、時間、力量）去（做某事）
brown-bag〔ˋbraʊnˋbæg〕v.（將酒類、食物等）自家裏帶來（到餐館、俱樂部、辦公室等地）

> *Dear Michelle,*
>
> *Here is hoping that your birthday will be shimmering bright, with joy and laughter from morning till night.*
>
> *Your loving husband*

親愛的蜜雪兒：

　　願妳的生日，閃閃發亮，伴隨著喜悅和歡笑，從天明到日落。

愛妳的先生上

** shimmer〔ˋʃɪmɚ〕v. 閃閃發亮

Paul ,

Can you believe that you will be 30 next month? In honor of your moving out of the twenties, we are giving you a big party.

Your friends

保羅：

你能相信你下個月就滿三十歲了嗎？為了慶祝你脫離二十歲，我們要為你舉行一個大派對。

你的朋友　上

My sweetheart ,

Once upon a time , there lived a little girl. And tomorrow she will be 20 years old. Do you know who she is?

Your boyfriend

我的甜心：

很久很久以前，有個可愛的小女孩。明天她就要滿二十歲了。妳知道她是誰嗎？

妳的男友　上

Sally,

Happy birthday to an attractive, intelligent, sophisticated and all-around splendid person.

David

莎莉：

祝福一位美麗迷人、聰明大方、有教養又倍受讚嘆的可人兒，生日快樂。

大衛

** attractive〔əˈtræktɪv〕*adj.* 迷人的
intelligent〔ɪnˈtɛlədʒənt〕*adj.* 聰明的
sophisticated〔səˈfɪstɪˌketɪd〕*adj.* 有教養的

Dear Steven,

There's been an awful mistake! It was my birthday I wanted to forget! Belated birthday greetings!

Eric

親愛的史迪夫：

真是個天大的錯誤！我只想忘掉自己的生日！（却連你的生日也忘了）雖然遲了一點，還是祝你生日快樂。

艾利克上

My little baby,

Here's hoping each moment all through the days will glitter and sparkle with everything gay. Yes, here's hoping a radiant day is in view, shining with goodness especially for you!

Love you
Andy

我的小寶貝：

　　願妳生命中的每一刻，都閃耀著萬物的欣喜。是的，希望燦爛的一天即將到來，為妳發出亮麗的光芒。

愛妳

安迪上

** glitter〔'glɪtɚ〕v. 發光
　 sparkle〔'spɑrkḷ〕v. 閃耀
　 gay〔ge〕adj. 欣喜的
　 radiant〔'redɪənt〕adj. 光明的；燦爛的

Dear Mom,

　　Warm wishes on your birthday.
I wish that I could be there to
celebrate it with you, but that is
impossible.　I send along my love
and affection.　I am also sending
a little gift.　I hope you like it.
Take care!

Your son,
Mick

親愛的媽媽：

　　獻給您溫馨的生日祝福。我希望我
能夠在那兒，和您一起慶祝，但那是不
可能的事。獻上我對您的愛與感情。我
也送上一份小禮物，希望您喜歡它。多
照顧自己！

您的兒子
密克上

** impossible〔ɪmˋpɑsəbḷ〕*adj.* 不可能的
　　send〔sɛnd〕*v.* 寄送　　***take care*** 小心；注意

Dear Joe,

Well, another year has gone by. I can remember clearly when you could sit on my knee. I hope you have a happy birthday. You can use the money any way you like. Your father and I love you very much.

Your mommy

親愛的喬：

一年又過去了。我可以清楚地記得，你還小得可以坐在我膝上的情景。希望你有一個愉快的生日。你可以隨意使用這筆錢。你父親和我都非常愛你。

你的媽咪上

go by 過去　　remember〔rɪˈmɛmbɚ〕*v.* 記得
knee〔ni〕*n.* 膝蓋

Dear Adam,

A happy birthday kiss for you! This little gift is just a token of my love and devotion to you. I love you very much. I will give you this as your present, but your real present will have to wait until tonight.

Your loving
Rebecca

親愛的亞當:

送你一個快樂的生日之吻!這份小禮物,只是我對你的愛情和忠誠的象徵。我非常地愛你。我先送你這張卡片做為生日禮物,但真正的禮物,今天晚上再送給你。

愛你的
麗蓓嘉上

** present〔'prɛznt〕n. 禮物
devotion〔dɪ'voʃən〕n. 忠誠;摯愛
wait〔wet〕v. 等待

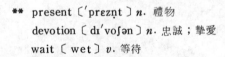

Unit
4

New-Arrival-Cards
嬰兒誕生賀卡

≪ New baby！≫

新生命的來臨，是每個家庭的大事。當你收到一封可愛的嬰兒誕生通知卡（ *announcement card* ）時，記得也要回寄一張祝賀卡喔！你也可以準備一份小禮，作為小寶貝的**見面禮**（ *welcome gift* ）。如果對方一直想要個男孩，却生了個女嬰，你可以這句話來安慰他們：“ *Girls are as good as boys to-day!* ”（在今天，男孩女孩一樣好呢！）

😊 小男孩 😊

☆ Congratulations on the birth of your son.　　　　　恭喜你們一舉得男。

☆ Congratulations on *the arrival of your baby*.　　　　恭賀小生命的來臨。

☆ We bid a warm welcome to your new baby.　　　　　我們熱忱歡迎你的小寶寶。

☆ Warm congratulations on your new baby boy.　　　　衷心祝福新誕生的小男孩。

**

arrival〔ə'raɪv!〕 *n.* 到達（的人或物）

☆ We are sending a little gift *for your new arrival*. / 我們寄上薄禮，給你們新誕生的小寶寶。

☆ We can't believe that you are now a father. Congratulations. / 眞不敢相信你做爸爸了。恭喜。

☆ We are wishing you joy and wonder and a little sleep. / 我們願你快樂，喜悅，並且稍作休息。

☆ Feeling proud and happy？ You have the right to be with you brand new baby boy. / 覺得驕傲，快樂嗎？有了新的小寶寶，你有權這麼做的。

☆ I can't wait to see your new son！ / 我等不及要看你的新生兒。

☆ Dad must be *bursting with* pride. / 爹地一定充滿了驕傲。

☆ Your new grandson is a real lucky boy. / 你的孫子是個幸運的男孩。

☆ We hope that your new son grows up healthy and strong. / 我們希望你的小男嬰，長得健康强壯。

☆ You two will make wonderful parents. Your son is a lucky boy. / 你們兩位會成爲很棒的父母，你們的兒子會是幸運的小孩。

☆ What a joy it is to raise children． Congratulations. / 撫育小孩樂趣無窮。恭喜。

** ─────────────────────

wonder〔'wʌndɚ〕 *n.* 奇蹟；奇事；驚奇
brand-new〔'brænd,nju〕 *adj.* 嶄新的；初生的　　*be burst with* 充滿

☆ *How does it feel* to be new parents ?	做父母的滋味如何？
☆ I hear that he is as cute as can be.	我聽說他可愛極了。
☆ Before you know it he will be *asking for* the keys to the car. Enjoy these times while you can.	很快地，他就會向你要車鑰匙了。好好享受這之前的時光吧。
☆ Does he look more like his dad or his mom？	他看起來像爸爸，還是像媽媽？
☆ We can imagine how proud both of you must be.	我們可以想像得到，你們必定感到十分驕傲。
☆ I can't wait to see the new little tyke, as well as the new parents.	我等不及要看小鬼和新升格的父母了！

😊 小女孩 😊

☆ Congratulations on the birth of your daughter.	恭喜小女孩的誕生。
☆ Congratulations on your new baby.	恭喜小寶貝的來到。

---

raise〔rez〕*v*. 栽培；撫養　　**tyke**〔taɪk〕*n*.〔俗〕小孩子；頑皮的兒童

☆ We are sending a welcome present to the little newcomer.

我們寄上一個歡迎禮物，給新來的小生命。

☆ There is nothing so beautiful as the creation of a new life.

世間最美好的事，莫過於新生命的誕生。

☆ We wish you the best with your new little girl.

謹以摯誠，祝福你和小寶寶。

☆ *I know that you had been hoping for a boy.* But a girl is as good as a boy.

我知道你一直想要一個男孩。但是男孩、女孩一樣好。

☆ It is such a joy to begin a family.

開始建立一個家庭是多麼令人喜悅的事。

☆ We share your happiness and wish you good luck with your new girl.

我們分享了你們的喜悅，並祝福小女孩。

☆ Girls are made of sugar and spice and everything nice.

女孩是蜜糖，香料和一切美好的事物所做成的。

☆ Congratulations！Your new granddaughter is a lucky girl.

恭喜！你新誕生的孫女是個幸運兒。

☆ I hope that she grows up to be a wonderful woman *just like her mother.*

願她長大後，成爲一個美麗的女人，就像她母親一樣。

---

newcomer〔'nju͵kʌmə〕*n.* 新來者　　creation〔krɪ'eʃən〕*n.* 創造；萬物

cute〔kjut〕*adj.* 可愛嬌小的　　spice〔spaɪs〕*n.* 香料；趣味

Sample Cards for New Arrivals

嬰兒誕生賀卡範例

把您的祝福包裝起來

Dear Mike and May,
　　We will make a trip to the hospital
to see the new born and the mother.
Take care !
　　　　　　　Jessie and Andy

親愛的麥克和玫：
　　我們將到醫院去探望新生兒和母親。請多保重！
　　　　　　　　　潔西和安迪上

Dear Grace,
　　We rejoice with you and wish
your daughter a long and happy
and meaningful life !
　　　　　　　Lily

親愛的萬麗絲：
　　我們為妳感到高興，並祝福妳的女兒長命百歲，有一個幸
福、快樂、且有意義的人生。
　　　　　　　　　莉莉上

** rejoice〔rɪˈdʒɔɪs〕*v.* 歡喜

Dear Bob and Nancy,

We were glad to hear that Nancy finally delivered her child. And now you have a beautiful baby girl. What a beautiful name you have given her. We hear that she's just as cute as a bug's ear! We wish you joy and happiness and a little sleep in the coming year ahead. Let us know if there is anything that we can do.

Your Dad and Mom

親愛的鮑伯和南茜：

真高興聽說南茜終於產下一子。現在你們有一個美麗的小女兒了。她有一個好迷人的名字。她真是可愛極了。我們祝福你們在未來一年充滿快樂，並保有一些睡眠時間。如果有任何地方，我們幫得上忙，請告訴我們。

你的爸和媽

** deliver〔dɪ'lɪvɚ〕v. 生產；分娩
as cute as a bug's ear 可愛極了；非常可愛

Unit  —— *Anniversary Cards* ——

周年賀卡

≪ **Happy Anniversary !** ≫

　　歐美人將**結婚紀念日**（ *wedding anniversary* ）賦予各種不同的名稱，如一週年則稱爲**紙婚**（ *paper anniversary* ），二週年則稱爲**棉布婚**（ *cotton anniversary* ），年份越久,則代表的名稱也越堅硬，表示婚姻維繫的歷久彌堅。到了五十週年則稱爲**金婚**（ *golden anniversary* ），當然最難得的，就是結婚七十五週年，稱爲**鑽石婚**（ *diamond anniversary* ）。

☺ 祝賀父母結婚紀念 ☺

☆ On your wedding anniversary:
　Love joins our present with
　the past and the future.

祝賀你們的結婚周年紀念日:
愛連結我們的過去，現在和
未來。

☆ A wish for your *golden anniversary.*

祝賀你們的金婚紀念日。

☆ For every lovely yesterday
　you've shared, you're wished
　and even lovelier tomorrow.

曾經共享的甜蜜往事，將使
你們的未來更美好。

＊＊

　future〔'fjutʃɚ〕*n.* 未來

☆ Congratulations to two wonderful parents on your wedding anniversary.

祝賀兩位最好的父母結婚周年紀念日。

☆ I feel lucky to have parents that stay together through *the ups and downs*. Congratulations.

我感到幸運，有兩位父母相伴度過人生起伏。恭喜。

☆ A happy anniversary wish from your loving son.

愛兒謹祝結婚周年快樂。

☆ I hope that my marriage lasts as long as yours has.

希望我的婚姻能和你們的一樣持久。

☺ 祝賀晚輩結婚紀念 ☺

☆ For two dear children: A happy home is built on love.

兩位親愛的孩子：愛是快樂家庭的基石。

☆ Wishing you both a happy anniversary.

祝你們倆有個快樂的結婚周年紀念日。

☆ Happy anniversary to a couple of *red hot lovers*.

祝熱戀的佳偶，結婚周年快樂。

☆ We are so proud of both of you. Happy anniversary.

我們為你們感到驕傲。結婚周年快樂。

☆ We knew that your marriage would last.

我們知道你們的婚姻將天長地久。

---

ups and downs 喻人生起伏　couple〔'kʌpl̩〕*n.* 一對

☆ This happy occasion is shared
　by all who love you.

讓深愛你們的人，分享這快
樂的時刻。

☆ Our best wishes on your first
　anniversary.

在你們結婚一週年，獻上我
們最誠摯的祝福。

☆ This is the first anniversary
　in a long line of anniversaries
　to come. Congratulations.

這將是你們無數結婚紀念日
的第一個。恭喜。

😊 夫妻之間 😊

☆ Happy anniversary, dear. With
　love on our anniversary.

周年快樂，親愛的。讓愛伴
隨著我們的結婚紀念日。

☆ *With love* on our golden wedd-
　ing anniversary.

金婚紀念日，獻上我的愛。

☆ I am so proud of you.

我以你爲榮。

☆ This is *in appreciation of* all
　that you mean to me.

你對我的意義,盡在感謝中。

☆ I am so lucky to have a part-
　ner like you.

我眞幸運，能擁有像妳這般
的伴侶。

☆ Always being together is my
　greatest happiness.

與你長相左右，是我最大的
幸福。

---

occasion〔ə'keʒən〕*n.* 場合；時機
golden wedding anniversary 金婚紀念日
appreciation〔ə,priʃɪ'eʃən〕*n.* 感激　partner〔'partnɚ〕*n.* 伴侶

☆ You are, and have always been, the only one for me. I love you.

你是，而且一直都是，我唯一的愛。我愛你。

☆ We've made it *this far*. Let's have just as many more happy anniversaries.

我們共同走過這麼長的路。讓我們攜手度過更多快樂的周年紀念。

☆ Honey, we always know each other's mind. I love you.

蜜糖，我們一直是心心相印的。我愛妳。

☆ Although your hairs have become gray, your *softness and sentiment* are still in my mind.

雖然妳已見白頭，但妳的似水柔情依然在我心中。

☆ On our wedding anniversary, I want to say: You are my *first love* forever.

在我們的結婚紀念日,我要對妳說：妳是我永遠的初戀。

☻ 祝賀朋友結婚紀念 ☻

☆ Congratulations on your anniversary !

恭賀結婚周年！

☆ Congratulations on your cotton wedding anniversary.

恭賀棉婚紀念日。

☆ May your anniversary *be filled with joy*.

願你們的結婚周年紀念，充滿喜悅。

✻✻

cotton wedding anniversary 棉婚（二週年）
be filled with 充滿

☆ We wish you many more anniversaries — each happier than
the one before.　　　　　　願你們擁有更多的周年紀念，
　　　　　　　　　　　　　而且一次比一次快樂。

☆ *Grow old and happy together.*　　願你們白頭偕老。

☆ Best wishes to you on your
anniversary.　　　　　　誠摯地祝福你們結婚周年快
　　　　　　　　　　　　樂。

☆ Congratulations to two dear
friends on your wedding anniversary.　　　　　　祝賀兩位親愛的朋友，結婚
　　　　　　　　　　周年快樂。

☆ Congratulations from your friends
on your paper anniversary.　　老友們一同祝賀你們紙婚周
　　　　　　　　　　　　　年快樂。

☆ We always admire your *love
story.*　　　　　　我們總是羨慕你倆的愛情故
　　　　　　　　　　事。

☺ 祝賀公司周年慶 ☺

☆ Congratulations on ten great
years of business.　　　恭賀十年來輝煌的業績。

☆ This business has lasted longer
than most marriages. Congratulations.　　　　　　您的事業比大多數婚姻還持
　　　　　　　　　　久。恭喜您。

☆ Wishing you *future success* and
happiness.　　　　　祝福你鴻圖大展，幸福快樂。

❋❋─────────────────────

paper anniversary 紙婚周年紀念（一周年）

☆ Happy anniversary! I knew that this store would make it.

周年快樂！我知道你的店會成功的。

☆ We wish you continued success. Happy anniversary.

祝你馬到成功。周年快樂。

☆ This business' success is testimony to your hard work.

事業成功是你勤奮工作的證明。

☆ Your hard work and diligence has *paid off*. Congratulations on your 10th anniversary.

你的努力勤奮換得豐收。祝賀你公司十週年慶。

☆ It seems like only yesterday that you opened this store.

彷彿昨天你才剛開張哩。

☆ You have done a good job on *running the business*. Congratulations on your anniversary.

經營生意，你幹得有聲有色。祝賀你公司周年慶。

☆ Sometimes I don't know if you are married to the store or me. But I am proud of your success. Happy anniversary.

有時候我不知你娶的是公司還是我。但我以你的成就為榮。周年慶快樂。

＊＊────────────────

testimony 〔'tɛstə,monɪ〕 *n.* 證言；證據

diligence 〔'dɪlədʒəns〕 *n.* 勤勉   *run a business* 經營生意

Sample Cards for Anniversary

周年賀卡範例

把您的祝福包裝起來

Darling,
　　You have been the best
wife and mother that a man
could ask for. I am proud
of you.

　　　　　　　　Kids' Dad

親愛的：

　　妳是男人心目中，最好的賢妻和良母。我為妳感到驕傲。

　　　　　　　　　　孩子的爸

Dear May and George,
　　We congratulate you on
your years spent together
and wish you success in
the years to come.

　　　Your friend Jessie

親愛的玫和喬治，

　　恭喜你們共度了這麼多年的美好時光，祝你們事事順心如意。

　　　　　　　　你們的朋友潔西　上

Dear Charlie,

I know that our future anniversaries will be better than all of the previous ones. I love you.

       Betty

親愛的查理：

  我知道我們未來的結婚紀念日，將會一年比一年更好。我愛你。

         貝蒂　上

** previous〔'prɪvɪəs〕*adj.* 先前的

Dear Miss Chen,

The success of your business is a tribute to your hard work and good business sense. Congratulations!

    David Wang

親愛的陳小姐：

  您的事業有成，正是您努力和商業頭腦的明證。恭喜您！

         王大衛　上

** tribute〔'trɪbjut〕*n.* 讚詞；表尊敬的行為

For two special parents，

*You have shown what love is all
about through special ways you've shared,
with wise advice you've offered and in
tender ways you've cared. You were always there when needed ; always willing
to help out. Happy anniversary !*

Your sons,
Alen and Adam

獻給兩位特別的父母：

　　你們以共有的特殊方式，明智的忠告、和
溫柔的關懷，證明了什麼是愛。在我們需要的
時候，你們總是伸出援手陪伴我們。結婚周年
快樂！

你們的兒子
亞倫和亞當　上

** advice〔əd'vaɪs〕 *n.* 忠告

Unit  ——————*Gift Cards*——————

禮 卡

《 **It's for you.** 》

　　禮卡（ *gift cards* ）多半是附在禮物上面，一起致送的。上面主要是表明爲什麼要送給對方這份禮物，如果這份小禮是對方早已渴望多時，你可寫上 “ *This is the gift that you have always said you wanted.* ”（這份禮物，是你一直想要的。）如果是大家一起合送的，則可寫上：“ *This is a present from all of us.* ”（這是我們大家一起送的。）

😃 禮卡常用語 😃

☆ It's especially for you.

這是特別給你的。

☆ This is just a small token of my appreciation.

這不過是代表我小小的感激之意。

☆ This is a present from the whole family.

這是來自全家人的禮物。

☆ I looked and looked for a present for you and finally decided on this.

我一直在找適合你的禮物，終於決定這份最合適。

---

token〔ˈtokən〕*n*. 表徵　　*decide on* 決定

☆ This present is from all of us.

這份禮物是我們全體合送的。

☆ It was really hard to *make up my mind* on what to get you. I finally decided on this.

要下決定，該買什麼給你才好，可眞不容易。終於我選了這份禮物。

☆ I thought this was "you" the moment I saw it.

我一瞧見它，就知道是最適合你不過了。

☆ I hope you like this.

我希望你會喜歡它。

☆ This is the shirt that you have always said you wanted.

這是你一直想要的那件襯衫。

☆ *I made this myself.*

這是我親手做的。

☆ If it doesn't fit you can always exchange it.

如果不合適的話，你可以去換。

☆ If you don't like the color you can take it back.

如果你不喜歡這種顏色，你可以拿回來。

☆ I am sorry I missed your birthday. Here is a little something for you.

抱歉錯過了你的生日。這是一點小小心意。

☆ This gift is for all the help you have given me.

這份禮物，是爲了感謝你所給予的一切協助。

☆ This is to show my appreciation for what you have done.

這是爲了表達，我對你所做的一切的感激之意。

** ──────────────

exchange〔ɪksˈtʃendʒ〕*v.* 交換

☆ I know that this isn't your birthday, but I just wanted to buy you something.

我知道今天不是你的生日，我只是想買些東西送你。

☆ *Here is a little gift for your graduation*.

這份小小的禮物，是為慶祝你畢業。

☆ The gift may be small, but there is a lot of love behind it.

禮輕情意重。

☆ Here is a little something to make the time go quicker while you are sick in bed.

這是你臥病在牀時，使時間加快腳步的小東西。

☆ This comes from all of those who love you.

這是所有愛你的人所送的。

☆ I like to buy things for you now and then.

我喜歡不時地買東西送你。

☆ This gift is a symbol of my love and affection.

這份禮物象徵我的愛情。

☆ Your tenderness and sweetness can only be repaid with this.

惟有這份禮物，才能回報你的溫柔與甜美。

---

graduation 〔͵grædʒʊˈeʃən〕*n.* 畢業   *now and then* 不時地

affection 〔əˈfɛkʃən〕*n.* 摯情   *repay with ~* 以~回報

☆ This is for you because I love you.

正因我愛你，才要送禮物給你。

☆ I want to give you something more substantial and permanent, like my love for you.

我想要給你一份更有價值，更永久的禮物，好比我對你的愛。

☆ Please accept this as *a token of my appreciation*.

請接受這份禮物，以代表我的感激之意。

☆ This is to show you that we appreciate all that you have done here.

這是爲了表示，我們感激你，爲這裡所做的一切。

☆ We really appreciate your help. Please accept this from all of us.

我們眞的很感激你的幫忙，請接受我們全體贈送的這份禮物。

☆ Here is a Valentine gift for you. I love you.

這是情人節禮物，我愛你。

☆ With this ring, I ask your hand in marriage.

戴上這只戒指，請妳嫁給我。

米米

substantial〔səbˈstænʃəl〕*adj*. 有價值的

permanent〔ˈpɝmənənt〕*adj*. 永久的

Valentine gift 情人節的禮物

Sample Gift Cards

把您的祝福包裝起來

Dear Emma,

Here is a little card I made myself. I hope you like it.

Clarie

親愛的艾瑪：

這是我親手做的卡片。希望妳會喜歡。

克萊兒上

Dear Janet,

Please accept this as a token of my love for you and my deepest affection.

Jim

親愛的珍娜：

請接受這份小禮，這是我對妳真情愛意的象徵。

吉姆

Dear Mary,

　This little gift is especially for you. You are so special to all of us. The moment that I saw it in the store, I knew that it was "you." If it is the wrong size, please let me know and I will exchange it. I hope you can wear this for your birthday party!

Your friend,
Lisa

親愛的瑪麗：

　這份小小的禮物是特別為妳而買的，對我們全體而言，你是如此的特別。當我在店裡瞧見它時，我知道它是再適合妳不過了。如果尺寸不合的話，請告訴我，我會拿去換。希望在妳生日派對時，妳能穿上它！

妳的朋友
麗莎

Unit **7** — *Thank-you-Cards* —
謝　卡

≪ **Thank you !** ≫

> 接受別人的幫忙或款待，要記得寫張卡片，表示你的感謝之意。卡片上的語氣要很誠懇，最好是**親筆**書寫。當然，別忘記給予朋友實質上的回報，你可在謝卡上寫著：" *I look forward to returning your hospitality.*"（我期待著能回報您的慇懃款待。）

☺ **感謝帮忙** ☺

☆ Thank you very much. That was thoughtful of you.　　十分感謝您。您眞是細心體貼。

☆ I know that you went out of your way. Thank you.　　我知道您已經給我額外的幫助了。謝謝。

☆ Your assistance was very much appreciated.　　非常感激您的幫助。

☆ Thank you for helping us move. *You were a big help.*　　謝謝您幫我們搬家。幫了我們一個大忙。

＊＊
thoughtful〔'θɔtfəl〕*adj*. 關心的；體貼的
assistance〔ə'sɪstəns〕*n*. 幫助　　appreciate〔ə'priʃɪˌet〕*v*. 感激
move〔muv〕*v*. 搬家

☆ We want to take you out to show our appreciation.

我們想請你吃一頓飯，以表達對你的感謝。

☆ Your efforts were appreciated very much.

您的幫忙備受感激。

☆ I don't think we could have done it without you. Thank you.

我想如果沒有你的幫忙，我們是不會成功的。謝謝你。

☆ If you ever need a hand, just call. *We owe you.*

不管什麼時候需要幫忙，儘管打電話來。我們欠您太多了。

☆ Without your help, the job would have never been completed.

那時候，要是沒有您的幫忙，工作便無法完成。

☆ Why don't you come by the house? The beer is *on me.* Thank you again for all that you have done.

何不順路到我家坐坐？我請你喝啤酒。再次謝謝你爲我們所做的一切。

☆ Allow us to repay you somehow. Your good deeds should be repaid.

請讓我們設法報答您。您的善行應該得到回饋。

---

take someone out 請某人吃飯　　appreciation〔ə,priʃɪ'eʃən〕*n.* 感謝
effort〔'ɛfət〕*n.* 努力；幫忙　　owe〔o〕*v.* 欠
come by（順路）造訪　　repay〔rɪ'pe〕*v.* 報答；回報
somehow〔'sʌm,haʊ〕*adv.* 以某種方法；設法

☆ One good deed deserves another.
We will pay you back. You can
count on it.

種善因，得善果。我們一定
要回報您的善意。

☆ Your thoughtfulness should not
go unrepaid.

您的體貼關注定會得到回報。

☆ Without you, it would have never
been possible. Thank you.

沒有你，事情根本就無法辦
好。謝謝你。

☆ Many thanks for the favor you
did for me!

謝謝你給我的一切幫助！

☆ Please accept my most cordial
thanks for your ***timely help***.

請接受我誠摯的謝意，感謝
您適時的幫忙。

☆ A friend in need is a friend
indeed! That's what I want
to say!

患難見眞情！這正是我要對
你說的！

☺ 感謝款待 ☺

☆ Somehow a simple " thank you "
doesn't really measure up to
what I'd like to say and give.

事實上，一句簡單的「謝謝」，
並不足以表達我內心的所思
所感。

☆ It was so thoughtful to invite
me to the party.

非常感謝您邀請我參加宴會。

---

deserve〔dɪ'zɝv〕*v.* 應得　　***measure up to*** 符合；達到

☆ *I had such a good time.* 　我度過一段美好的時光。

☆ I enjoyed the weekend with you so much. 　有妳伴我度週末，我非常開心。

☆ I'll always remember the wonderful time I had with you. 　我將永遠記得，我跟你共處的那一段美好日子。

☆ I was so happy to be able to see you. 　很高興能夠見到你。

☆ Thank you so much for the dinner the other night. 　謝謝您前幾天晚上的晚餐。

☆ Thank you for the hospitality that you showed my daughter. 　謝謝您招待我的女兒。

☆ Thank you for your hospitality *during my trip.* 　謝謝您在旅途中，給我的款待。

☆ You were so gracious to extend such warm hospitality. 　您真是很和藹、親切，給與那麼熱烈的款待。

☆ If you are ever in Seattle, please let me extend you the same hospitality as you extended to me. 　要是您到西雅圖來，請讓我也像您曾經接待我一樣地款待您。

**

hospitality〔,hɑspɪ'tælətɪ〕*n.* 好客；款待
trip〔trɪp〕*n.* 旅行；遠足　　gracious〔'greʃəs〕*adj.* 和藹的；親切的
extend〔ɪk'stɛnd〕*v.* 致；給

☆ You were more than a hostess. Your hospitality will be remembered.　　您這位女主人當得太好了。您的慇懃招待，我將永記於心。

☆ Your hospitality will be repaid.　　您的親切款待會得到回報。

☆ I wish there were more people in the world like yourself.　　但願世界上能有多一些，像您這樣的人。

☆ You should feel proud about the way you treat other people.　　您應該以自己對待別人的方式爲榮。

☆ Thank you for your hospitality.　　謝謝你的慇懃款待。

☆ I warmly appreciate your hospitality.　　眞心感激您的熱心招待。

☺ 感謝別人的道賀 ☺

☆ Your kind words are greatly appreciated.　　非常感激您的祝賀。

☆ How can I ever thank you enough.　　我無法表達心中的感激。

☆ It made me so happy that you remembered my birthday.　　你記得我的生日，令我十分高興。

☆ **Give my best** to all the family.　　代我向家人問候。

☆ You are a very nice person to say the things that you did.　　給予我如此的祝福，您眞是位好人。

---

hostess〔ˈhostɪs〕*n*. 女主人

☆ You words were so kind!   你的話語，十分中聽呢！

☆ You are much too kind.   您真是很仁慈。

☆ I don't deserve such praise   我不值得您如此的稱讚。不
from you. But thank you.   過，還是要謝謝您。

☆ Your words *mean a lot* to me.   您的話，對我意義深遠。

☆ It was unnecessary for you   您所說的讚美，真令我感到
to *go out of your way* to say   不好意思，您大可不必這麼
such things.   費心的。

☆ Thank you for sharing the joy   感謝您與我們一同分享新生
of our new baby.   兒的喜悅。

☆ I only wish that more young   我真希望有更多的年輕人，
people were as well-mannered   能夠像你一樣的有禮貌。
as you are.

☆ Your parents have raised you   你的父母親把你教養得很好。
well.

☆ It takes a person of special   您對我的祝賀，正顯示出您
character to say the words   的崇高品格。
that you said to me.

☆ My hat is off to you for your   我為您的美言，脫帽致謝。
kind words.

＊＊ ――――――――――――――

praise〔prez〕*n.* 讚美
well-mannered〔'wɛl'mænəd〕*adj.* 有禮貌的；舉止得體的
raise〔rez〕*v.* 養育；教養　　special〔'spɛʃəl〕*adj.* 特殊的；特別的
character〔'kærəktə〕*n.* 個性；品德

☆ The bliss of our engagement would not seem complete without the thoughful card you sent us.

若沒有你寄來的訂婚祝福卡，我們的喜悅將不完整。

☆ We are very grateful for your congratulations and good wishes.

對於您的祝賀與祝福，我們十分感激。

☆ Thank you for your congratulations. I fear I do not deserve them.

謝謝你的祝賀。我深感慚愧。

😊 其他場合 😊

☆ It was so kind of you to come and visit me at the hospital.

您真好，到醫院來探望我。

☆ You are a kind prince for coming to visit me while I was ill.

在我生病時來看我，你真像是一位好心的王子。

☆ Thank you very much for the gifts and cards while I was ill.

非常謝謝您在我臥病時，所送的禮物及卡片。

☆ Your card and gift were really appreciated. Thank you.

非常感謝您的卡片及禮物。謝謝。

☆ *Your taking time* out from your busy schedule was duly appreciated.

很感謝您，能從百忙中抽空出來。

---

prince〔prɪns〕*n.* 王子　　schedule〔'skɛdʒul〕*n.* 時間表
duly〔'djulɪ〕*adj.* 十分地

☆ Thank you for your kind wedding present.

感謝你送的那份美好的結婚賀禮。

☆ Your wedding gift was received *with great pleasure*.

很高興收到您送的結婚賀禮。

☆ You are so kind for sending us a gift on our wedding day.

您真好，在我們結婚當天送來了禮物。

☆ Your gift was exactly what we needed. Thank you very much.

您的禮物恰好是我需要的。十分謝謝您。

☆ Your gift will be *put to good use*. It is perfect for our new house.

您的禮物會被好好使用。它很適合我們的新房子。

☆ Your birthday present was great. I love it! Thank you!

你送的生日禮物很棒。我很喜歡！謝謝！

☆ Your gift was my favorite. Thank you very much.

我最喜歡你送的禮物。十分謝謝你。

☆ I don't know how I could have lived without the microwave oven. Thank you for your gift.

我真的不敢想像,沒有微波爐的日子，會是怎樣過的。謝謝你的禮物。

☆ Your kindness is too much. Thank you so much.

您的恩澤太深。我感激不盡。

☆ Your generosity is deeply appreciated.

深深感謝您的慷慨。

** ————————————————

microwave oven 微波爐　　generosity 〔͵dʒɛnəˈrɑsətɪ〕 *n.* 慷慨；寬大

Sample Thank-you Cards

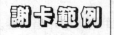

把您的祝福包裝起來

Dear Diana,

It made me so happy that you remembered my birthday. Your words were so kind!

Sylvia

親愛的黛安娜：

妳記得我的生日，真令我高興。妳的祝福是那麼親切！

西維亞

Dear Miss Wang,

I will always remember the time with you. If you are ever in my neighborhood, you have a place to stay. Thanks again!

Jane

親愛的王小姐：

我將永遠記得和妳共度的時光。如果妳到附近來，我將為妳安排住宿。再次向妳道謝！

** neighborhood〔ˈnebɚˌhʊd〕 *n.* 附近地區

Dear Mrs. Chang,

　　I wish there were a better word than thanks to express my appreciation for your help.

　　　　　　　　　　Ellen

親愛的張太太：

　　我真希望能找到比「謝謝」更好的字眼，來表達我對妳的謝意。

　　　　　　　　　　愛倫

** express 〔 ɪksˊprɛs 〕 *v.* 表達

Dear Andy,

　　Thank you for your lovely flowers. They helped cheer me up on several gloomy days!

　　　　　　　　　　Jessica

親愛的安迪：

　　謝謝你送來的可愛花朵。它們在許多晦暗的日子裡鼓舞了我。

　　　　　　　　　　潔西嘉

** ***cheer up*** 鼓舞　　gloomy 〔 ˊglumɪ 〕 *adj.* 晦暗的

Dear Mary,

Thank you for the warmest senti-ments which I know came from the heart!

Windy

親愛的瑪麗：

謝謝妳溫馨的情意，我知道它們來自妳的內心！

溫蒂上

＊＊ sentiment 〔 ′sɛntɪmənt 〕 *n.* 情意

Mike,

One of the best things about graduation was getting so many nice cards from my friends!

Your friend George

麥克：

畢業最棒的事之一，就是收到許多朋友的賀卡。

你的朋友　喬治上

Dear Mrs. Lee,

What a lovely evening we spent with you and Richard. We enjoyed the delicious dinner and good bridge game. I hope that you will soon be able to visit Taipei again and I look forward to returning your hospitality.

Diana

親愛的李太太：

我們和你及理查，共度了這麼美好的下午。我們享用了可口的晚餐和有趣的橋牌遊戲。我希望你們將很快地再到台北來，我將期待著回報你們的慇懃款待。

黛安娜上

** *bridge game* 橋牌遊戲

Dear Jane,

How sweet you are! I really appreciated your visit while I was in the hospital. I can't tell you how much better your visit made me feel. I am glad you took time out from your busy schedule. Your generosity is noted and appreciated. Thank you.

Mike

親愛的珍：

妳真是太好了！我十分感謝妳上次到醫院來探望我。我無法告訴妳，妳的慰問，使我感到何等的舒暢。很高興妳在百忙中，撥空來看我。感激妳的仁厚，我將永記心中。謝謝。

麥克上

**hospital 〔ˈhɑspɪtḷ〕 n. 醫院
generosity 〔ˌdʒɛnəˈrɑsətɪ〕 n. 仁厚；寬大

Unit **8** — *Invitation Cards* —
邀請卡

≪We welcome you！≫

一般的**邀請卡**（ *invitation cards* ）有正式和非正式之分。正式的邀請，則有一定的格式可尋，多用 *"We request the pleasure of your company..."* 這類句型開頭。非正式的邀請，語氣較爲活潑多變，只要言明邀請的目的，和時間、地點即可！若爲方便客人尋找，可在卡片中附上地圖（ *map* ）。

😃 生日派對 😃

☆ This is to inform you of a *surprise birthday party* at John Smith's house on the 7th of June at 4 in the afternoon.

謹通知你在六月七日下午四點，於約翰・史密斯家，將有一個驚喜生日派對。

☆ If you can't make it, please call John's wife at her place of work. (*Don't call the house*！) Her number is 123-4567。

如果你不克前來，請打電話至約翰妻子的辦公室給她。（別打到她家！）她的電話號碼是 123-4567。

**———————————

inform〔ɪnˈfɔrm〕 *v*. 通知
surprise birthday party 驚喜生日派對（不讓壽星知道）

☆ We are having a birthday party for John on July the 7th at around 4 in the afternoon.

我們將在七月七日下午約四點左右，為約翰舉行一個生日派對。

☆ We would love to have you join us.

我們很希望你能參加。

☆ You need not bring a gift.

你不需要帶禮物。

☆ Give us a call if you can't make it, otherwise we will expect you at the party.

如果你不能來，就打個電話給我們，否則我們會在派對上等你來。

☆ We are celebrating John's birthday with a big *masquerade party*.

我們將舉行一個化裝舞會，來慶祝約翰生日。

☆ There will be prizes for best costume.

我們將頒發「最佳服裝獎」。

☆ On the back of the inviation is a map of how to get to our place.

邀請卡的背面，有一張地圖，教你如何找到我們的地方。

☆ Please call to let us know if you are not coming.

如果你不來，請打電話通知我們。

☆ We'll see you at the party.

我們舞會上見。

---

masquerade party 化裝舞會
costume〔'kɑstjum〕*n.* 戲服；服裝

☆ *You are cordially invited* to attend a birthday brunch at the Smith residence on Saturday, July 7th at 11 o'clock in the morning.

我們誠摯地邀請你參加七月七日（星期六）上午十一點，在史密斯家舉行的生日早午餐會。

☆ Bring a friend if you like. *The more the merrier.*

可帶個朋友來，隨你喜歡。人愈多愈開心。

☆ *See you here* !

到時候見！

😊 一般宴會的邀請 😊

☆ Your presence is requested at a cocktail party.

希望你光臨雞尾酒會。

☆ We would like you to join us for a tea party.

我們希望你能參加我們的茶會。

☆ We are holding a masquerade party.

我們將舉行一個化裝舞會。

☆ *Come on over* and join us for a sock-hop.

過來參加我們的「襪子舞會」。

☆ You are cordially invited to a dinner party.

誠摯地邀請你參加晚宴。

---

cordially〔ˈkɔrdʒəlɪ〕*adv.* 眞誠地；誠摯地
brunch〔brʌntʃ〕*n.* 早午餐　　*cocktail party* 雞尾酒會
sock-hop〔ˈsɑkˌhɑp〕*n.* 不穿鞋，只著襪跳舞的舞會（盛行於美國高中生之間）

☆ The party starts at 6 P.M. 　　　宴會於下午六點開始。

☆ We start rocking and rolling 　　舞會於晚上九點正開始。
at 9 P.M. sharp.

☆ The fun starts at 8 o'clock 　　　餘興節目將從晚上八點開始。
in the evening.

☆ Please call and let us know 　　　如果你不來，請打電話通知
if you are not coming. 　　　　　我們。

☆ *Give us a ring* if you can't 　　　如果你無法參加，撥個電話
make it. 　　　　　　　　　　給我們。

☆ We are holding a dinner par- 　　我們將於星期天，於亞都飯
ty on Sunday at the Ritz Hotel. 店舉行一次晚餐會。

☆ We will be throwing a dinner 　　我們將為約翰舉行一次晚宴。
party *in John's honor*.

😊 野餐郊遊的邀請 😊

☆ Now that the weather is good, 　既然天氣很好，我們想舉行
we thought we would have a 　　一次野餐。
picnic.

☆ Please join us for a picnic in 　請加入我們在公園裡的野餐。
the park.

** ⎯⎯⎯⎯⎯⎯⎯⎯⎯⎯⎯⎯⎯⎯⎯⎯⎯⎯⎯⎯⎯⎯⎯⎯

rock and roll 跳搖滾舞　　*now that* 既然；因為
picnic〔'pɪknɪk〕*n.* 野餐

☆ We are *having a picnic* in the park.

我們將在公園辦一次野餐。

☆ On the back is a map of how to get to the picnic spot.

背面是一張圖，教你如何到野餐地點。

☆ We have drawn a map for those of you who don't know how to get to our house.

我們已替你們這些不知道我家怎麼走的人，畫好了地圖。

☆ Our house is a little difficult to find, so we put a map on the back.

我們家有點不好找，所以我們放了張地圖在背面。

☆ This picnic is pot-luck. Call me so we don't all bring the same thing.

這次野餐是自己帶食物來的便餐形式。打電話給我，這樣我們不會帶同樣的東西。

☆ To celebrate the coming of spring, we are *holding a picnic* in the mountains.

為慶祝春天的來臨，我們將在山區舉行一次野餐。

😃 邀請來訪小住 😃

☆ You are more than welcome to stay at our house.

非常歡迎你到我們家小住。

☆ We have more than enough room for you.

我們有充份的空間讓你居住。

＊＊

spot〔spɑt〕*n.* 地點　　pot-luck〔'pɑt,lʌk〕*n.* 便飯；現成菜飯
celebrate〔'sɛlə,bret〕*v.* 慶祝

☆ It would be no trouble *at all* to put you up.

讓你寄宿在此，一點也不麻煩。

☆ Please come by to see us.

請來看我們。

☆ We would love to see you. It has been so long.

已經過了這麼久了，我們很想見你。

☆ Leave room in your plans for a stay at our place.

在你的計畫裡留一些空檔，到我們這兒住一陣子。

☆ We would be honored if you would visit us.

如果你能來拜訪我們，是我們的光榮。

☆ *You should stay here with us.*

你應該來和我們一起住些時日。

⊙ 邀請參加聚會 ⊙

☆ *We request the honor of your presence* at the meeting.

敬邀您蒞臨這次聚會。

☆ Please join us for a meeting at the Allen's.

請參加我們在愛倫家的聚會。

☆ It has been so long since we last met.

自從我們上次見面後，至今已有好長一段時間了。

☆ Why don't we meet at the Big Beer for lunch.

我們在大啤酒屋吃頓午餐敍一敍吧。

**

request〔rɪ'kɛst〕*v.* 懇請

☆ You are asked to join this
meeting as it is of extreme
importance.

邀請你參加這個極度重要的
會議。

☆ If you could join us, it
would be wonderful.

如果你能來，那真是太好了。

☆ I would like to *get together*
with you on July 14 at 7P.M.
at the I R Restaurant.

我想在七月十四日下午七點，
與你在耶廬餐廳聚一聚。

☆ If you are unable to accept
this invitation, please RSVP.

如果你無法接受這項邀請，
請儘快回覆。

**

extreme〔ɪk'strim〕*adj.* 極端的
invitation〔ˌɪnvə'teʃən〕*n.* 邀請   ***RSVP*** 儘快回覆

Sample Invitation Cards

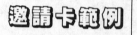

邀請卡範例

把您的祝福包裝起來

· ·

Dear Miss Chen ,
   It would give me great pleasure if
you would come to tea with me !

　　　　　　　　John Wang

親愛的陳小姐：

　　如果妳願與我共享下午茶，那將是我的榮幸！

　　　　　　　　　　　　王約翰

Dear Charlotte ,
   Just to remind you that we are
expecting you and Dick on the sixth.
Can't wait to see you.

　　　　　　　　Love,
　　　　　　　　Anita

親愛的夏綠蒂：

　　只是提醒你和狄克，我們都在等候6號聚會的來臨。真等不
及想見到你們。

　　　　　　　　　　　　愛你的

　　　　　　　　　　　　艾妮塔　上

Mr. and Mrs. John Smith
request the pleasure of
Mr. and Mrs. Paul Jones'
company at a
birthday party
on Saturday, the seventh of July
at eight o'clock
Lai Lai Sheraton
Taipei, Taiwan

　　約翰・史密斯夫婦謹訂於七月七日
（星期六），假台北市來來飯店，舉行
生日宴會，敬邀保羅・瓊斯夫婦大駕光
臨，屆時務必賞光。

** pleasure〔'plɛʒɚ〕*n.* 榮幸；賞光

Unit 9 ———— *Apology Cards* ————

道歉卡

≪ I am sorry! ≫

　　我們難免會因為犯錯或疏忽，而須向別人道歉。這時，就要立刻寄上**道歉卡片**（ *apology cards* ）。如果事過多時才寄出，則會顯得沒有誠意。在卡片中可以為你的過失或苦衷作解釋，但不要**強辯**，這樣反而會招致對方的反感。若真是自己的疏失，則不妨直言：" *It was all my fault.* "（這都是我的錯。）

☺ 為失約道歉 ☺

☆ *I am sorry for* forgetting our appointment.

我為忘記我們的約會感到抱歉。

☆ Please give me a chance to explain to you why I missed meeting you.

請給我一個機會，讓我向你解釋，為何我沒來見你。

☆ I *apologize for* missing our appointment.

我為沒赴我們的約會，向你道歉。

---

appointment〔ə'pɔɪntmənt〕*n.* 約會
apologize〔ə'pɑlə,dʒaɪz〕*v.* 道歉

☆ I hope you weren't too upset
at my missing our meeting.
It was *due to* circumstances
beyond my control.

我希望你沒因為我的失約而
太生氣。因為情況超乎了我
的控制。

☆ I am sorry, but I was held
up in traffic for 2 hours.

我很抱歉，我被交通阻塞困
住了兩小時。

☆ I apologize for making you
upset. Let me *make it up*
to you.

我很抱歉，使你生氣。讓我
們言歸於好吧。

☆ Is there any way that I can
make up for my forgetfulness?

有沒有辦法，讓我可以為我
的善忘彌補過失呢？

☆ You must be angry with me.
I don't blame you. The fact
is I just plain forgot about
our meeting.

你一定很氣我。我不怪你。
事實上，我是把我們的約會
忘了一乾二淨。

☆ I feel like a real heal. I
deserve 30 lashes. I am so
sorry.

我真的希望和你和解。我該
罰三十皮鞭。我真的很對不
起。

☆ Will you ever forgive my
absentmindedness? I want
to make it up to you.

你能原諒我的心不在焉嗎？
我想與你和解。

**　——————————————————

circumstance〔'sɝkəm,stæns〕*n.* 情形　　*make up* 和解；復合
heal〔hil〕*n.* 痊癒；和解　　lash〔læʃ〕*n.* 鞭撻
absentmindedness〔'æbsn̩t'maɪndɪdnɪs〕*n.* 心不在焉

☺ 爲傷某人的心道歉 ☺

☆ I am sorry for hurting your feelings the other day.

前幾天我傷了你的感情，我很抱歉。

☆ ***I had no idea that*** I was saying something that was painful. Please forgive my thoughtlessness.

我不知道那時說的話，會那麼令你痛苦。請原諒我的疏忽。

☆ I don't know how I could be so thoughtless.

我不知道，怎會如此不小心。

☆ Please give me a chance to make it up to you.

請給我個機會，讓我們和解。

☆ I feel really badly about hurting your feelings. I had no idea of the circumstance behind the gossip.

傷了你的心，我真的覺得很難過。我並不了解這閒言閒語背後的真象。

☆ This should teach me a lesson about ***saying the wrong thing at the wrong time***.

這應該給了我一個教訓，不要在不當的時機，說不當的話。

☆ I don't know how I could be so insensitive. I am sorry.

我不知我怎麼會如此遲鈍。我很抱歉。

**

thoughtless〔ˈθɔtlɪs〕*adj.* 不注意的；疏忽的
gossip〔ˈgɑsəp〕*n.* 閒話   insensitive〔ɪnˈsɛnsətɪv〕*adj.* 無感覺的

☆ I guess you have the right to be upset. I am sorry, though.

我想你有權利生氣。我還是很抱歉。

☆ I guess *my name is mud.*

我想我是信譽掃地了。

☆ You are very right to be angered with me. Please find it in your heart to forgive me.

你對我生氣是很對的。請你在心裡原諒我。

👹 為失禮道歉 👹

☆ I am sorry for being rude the other day.

我為那天的無禮，向你道歉。

☆ I am sorry. I just didn't know *what I was saying.*

我很抱歉，那天我不知道自己在說些什麼。

☆ I hope you can forgive my rudeness. I really *had no intention of* behaving that way.

希望你能原諒我的無禮。我那樣的舉動，實在並非有意。

☆ I sometimes get a little out of control when I drink. I hope you can forgive my behavior.

我喝酒時，有時會有點失去自制。希望你能寬恕我的行為。

----

intention〔ɪn'tɛnʃən〕*n.* 意圖；目的
behave〔bɪ'hev〕*v.* 舉動

☆ I was really *out of line* for saying those things to you. I hope you can see my point of view on the matter.

我對你說那些話，實在太不像樣了。希望你能了解我對那件事的想法。

☆ Sometimes the words just come out wrong. I apologize for the comments.

有時就是會說錯話。我為那些批評向你致歉。

☆ I really regret the things that I said. Please let me make it up to you.

我真的為我所說的話，感到後悔。讓我與你和解吧。

☆ I guess *I put my foot in my mouth*. Please let me take you to lunch to make it up to you.

我想我失言了。請讓我與你共進午餐，和好如初吧。

☆ Please let me explain my feelings more completely. I am afraid that they sounded rude, but I really meant no harm.

請讓我更詳盡地解釋我的感覺。我擔心它們聽起來很魯莽，但我沒有惡意。

☆ I really don't want this incident to come between us.

我實在不希望我們之間發生這種事。

---

out of line 行為不檢　　comment〔ˈkɑmɛnt〕*n.* 談論；批評
put one's foot in one's mouth 說話不謹慎
incident〔ˈɪnsədənt〕*n.* 事件

☺ 爲犯錯致歉 ☺

☆ I am sorry. I made a mistake.　　　我很抱歉。我犯了錯。

☆ *It was all my fault.*　　　這都是我的錯。

☆ You will have to forgive me.
  I make mistakes sometimes.

你一定得原諒我。我有時會
犯錯。

☆ Sometimes I have to make a
  mistake before I know what is
  the right thing to do.

有時在了解怎樣做才對之前,
我總先犯個錯。

☆ I am completely *at fault*. I
  am deeply sorry for my mis-
  judgment.

我完全錯了。我爲我的判斷
錯誤深表歉意。

☆ When I make mistakes, I need
  people like you to tell me.
  Otherwise I won't know.

當我作錯事,我需要像你這
樣的朋友來告訴我,否則我
將不知道。

☆ I am grateful for friends like
  you who tell me when I make
  a mistake.

像你這樣的朋友,能在我犯
錯時,告訴我,我非常感激。

☆ *There is no way* to erase what
  I have done. I am sorry.

我所做的事,已是無法抹去
了。我很抱歉。

** ─────────

at fault 罪有應得;失措　　misjudgment〔mɪs'dʒʌdʒmənt〕*n.* 判斷錯誤
grateful〔'gretfəl〕*adj.* 感激的　　erase〔ɪ'res〕*v.* 抹去

☆ I wish I could go back and change what I have done.

但願我能回到當時，改變我所做的事實。

☆ I will try to learn from this mistake.

我將試著從這次的錯誤，學得一些教訓。

🙂 為爭吵致歉 🙂

☆ I am sorry about our misunderstanding. *It was all my fault.*

我對我們之間的誤解，覺得很抱歉。這都是我的錯。

☆ I would like to get together with you and *talk* our disagreement *out*.

我想和你見面，將我們的爭論說個清楚。

☆ We shouldn't let a thing like this stand in the way of our friendship.

我們不應該讓這種事，成為我們友誼的障礙。

☆ Let's not let a disagreement destroy our good friendship.

我們不要讓意見不合毀了我們的友情。

☆ I am sorry for what I said. It was my fault.

我對我所說的致歉。這是我的錯。

☆ I don't want to lose your friendship *over* a thing like this.

我不想因為這麼一件事，而失去了你的友誼。

**

misunderstanding〔͵mɪsʌndɚ'stændɪŋ〕*n.* 誤會　　***talk out*** 談個明白

disagreement〔͵dɪsə'grimənt〕*n.* 意見不合　　destroy〔dɪs'trɔɪ〕*v.* 毀壞

☆ Let's get together and talk it out in a civilized manner.

讓我們聚一聚，以文雅的態度把事情談個明白。

☆ We have had disagreements before. We can work out this one too.

我們曾經意見不合過。這次我們也能解決。

☆ Let me *make* it *up* to you *with* a dinner.

讓我以一頓晚餐彌補你吧。

☆ We can still be friends. Everyone has their disagreements.

我們仍然可以是朋友。每個人都會有意見不和的時候。

☺ 其它狀況 ☺

☆ I am sorry I haven't written. There is really no excuse.

我很抱歉沒能寫信給你。這實在是不可原諒。

☆ I am sorry for my long silence. But you have been *on my mind*.

我爲我許多次的沈默，向你道歉。但是你一直在我心中。

☆ I promise that I will write more *in the future*.

我答應你，以後我會更勤加寫信。

☆ My silence is unforgivable. I am truly sorry.

我的沈默眞是無可原諒。我實在很抱歉。

**

civilized〔'sɪvḷ,aɪzd〕*adj.* 有禮貌的
unforgivable〔,ʌnfɚ'gɪvəbḷ〕*adj.* 不可原諒的

☆ I have been thoughtless in not writing to you. I will correct my behavior.

一直沒寫信給你，是我的疏忽。我一定改正。

☆ I am truly sorry for denting your car. I will pay for it.

把你的車子撞凹了，眞是對不起。我會賠償你的。

☆ I am sorry for breaking your vase. It was clumsy of me.

我很抱歉打破了你的花瓶。我眞是笨手笨脚的。

☆ I promise that I will take better care of your things. I apologize for the condition *in which* I returned them to you.

我保證會更加小心地照料你的東西。把你的東西弄成這樣，我實在很抱歉。

☆ There is no excuse for my clumsiness. I will pay for the damage.

我的笨拙實在不可原諒。我會賠償你的損失的。

☆ I promise that it will never happen again.

我保證這永遠不會再發生。

**　——————————

dent〔dɛnt〕v. 弄成凹痕　　clumsy〔ˈklʌmzɪ〕adj. 笨拙的
damage〔ˈdæmɪdʒ〕n. 損失；傷害

Sample Apology Cards

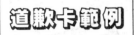

道歉卡範例　　　　　　把您的祝福包裝起來

Dear Jane,
　　It was thoughtless and rude of me
to say such things. I am really sorry.

Nicola

親愛的珍：

　　我真是又大意又無禮，才會說那樣的話。我真的很抱歉。

妮可拉　上

thoughtless〔`θɔtlɪs`〕*adj.* 輕率的；大意的
rude〔rud〕*adj.* 粗魯的；沒教養的；無禮的

To my lovely Jessica,
　　I hope you can forgive my
clumsiness. Please give me a
chance to make it up to you!

Poor Charlie

給我可愛的潔西嘉：

　　希望妳能原諒我的笨手笨腳。請給我一個機會來補償妳！

可憐的查理　上

Dear Miss Wang,

    I am sorry that I hurt your feelings the other day. I really didn't know what I was saying. Please forgive me!

David Lee

親愛的王小姐：

    前幾天，傷了妳的心，我感到很抱歉。我真不知道當時在說些什麼。請妳原諒我！

李大衛　上

To my pretty and kind Ann,

    I really apologize for breaking your new vase. Just call me "butter-fingers". I feel so badly about it.

Your butter-fingers

給我美麗善良的安：

    我真的要向妳道歉，因為我打破了妳的新花瓶。妳就叫我「笨手笨腳的呆瓜」好了。我真的很難過。

你笨手笨腳的呆瓜　上

** butter-fingers〔ˈbʌtə͵fɪŋɡəz〕 *n.* 易將手中物滑落的人

My Dear Christina,

I am sorry about the misunder-
standing that we had. I hope that this
doesn't stand in the way of our great
friendship. I must admit, it was all
my fault and you are right to be an-
gry. Can you ever forgive me?

Your faithful Jason

親愛的克莉斯汀娜：

　　對於我們的誤會，我覺得很抱歉。希
望這不會妨礙了我們美好的友誼。我必須
承認，這都是我的錯，你生氣是對的。你
能原諒我嗎？

　　　　　妳忠實的傑森　上

** ***in the way*** 妨礙；阻礙
friendship〔'frɛndʃɪp〕 *n.* 友誼

Dear Mr. Wu ,

　　I am so sorry for missing our appointment. I know you must have been upset. It was all due to my forgetfulness. I hope that you can forgive me. Let me make it up to you by buying you a lunch. I will call you later in the week.

James

親愛的吳先生：

　　很抱歉我失約了。我知道您一定很生氣。這都是因為我的健忘。希望您能原諒我。讓我請您吃午餐來補償您吧。這個星期五、六我會打電話給您。

詹姆士

＊＊ miss〔mɪs〕v. 錯失
upset〔ʌp'sɛt〕adj. 生氣的；煩亂的

Unit 10 — *Sympathy-Cards* —
慰問卡

≪ **Get well soon！** ≫

　　朋友的家人去世了，這時你的**慰問卡**（ *sympathy card* ）必須以表達懇切的關懷與哀思爲主，句子不宜過長。另外，致送的時間亦越快越好。若是寫卡片給病中的朋友，則以**幽默風趣**（ *humor* ）爲主，儘量讓朋友感到開心，希望他（她）能早日復元（ *Get well soon！* ）。此外，還可以準備一些笑話或點心，連同卡片一起帶去。

😃 弔唁慰問 😃

☆ With heartfelt sympathy for you and your family at this time of sorrow.

在這個哀傷的時刻，謹向你及你的家人致上慰問之意。

☆ I send my love and my deepest sympathy to you and your family.

謹向您及您的家人，致上我的關愛與最深的慰問。

☆ I was deeply grieved to learn of the sudden death of your husband.

知道你先生突然過世，我非常悲傷

**

heartfelt〔ˈhɑrt,fɛlt〕*adj.* 至誠的　　sympathy〔ˈsɪmpəθɪ〕*n.* 慰問

☆ I can only imagine how much you will miss your mother.

我能想像得到，你將多麼思念你的母親。

☆ I wish I knew how to console you *at this time of sorrow*.

但願我知道，如何在這悲哀的時刻中安慰你。

☆ My heart is filled with sorrow for you.

我心中爲你充滿了哀傷。

☆ He will be missed by many.

他將爲許多人所懷念。

☆ She meant so much to all who knew her.

對所有熟識她的人而言，她是多麼重要。

☆ If there is anything that I can do for you, please don't hesitate to let us know.

假如有我可以爲你效勞的地方，請不要猶豫，讓我們知道。

☆ I was shocked when I heard the news.

我聽到消息時，甚感驚愕。

☆ I can only begin to imagine the pain that you must be in.

我能想像得到，你所承受的痛苦。

☆ If you need to talk or if you need anything, just let me know.

如果你需要找人傾訴，或有任何需要，就讓我知道。

✱✱────────────

console〔kən'sol〕*v.* 安慰   hesitate〔'hɛzə,tet〕*v.* 遲疑；猶豫

☆ *She meant so much to us all.* 　　她對我們全體是那麼重要 。

☆ I only regret that I didn't spend more time with her. 　　我只是後悔 ，沒有花更多時間與她相聚 。

☆ I am sorry for not writing sooner，but I have been out of the country and have just learned of his death. 　　我很抱歉沒有早點寫信 ，但我人在國外 ，剛剛才知道他去世的消息 。

☆ *It seems so unfair sometimes.* 　　有時人生似乎太不公平 。

☆ If only I could be there with you at this time. 　　要是這次我能前去和你在一起就好了 。

☆ There is pain in my heart at the news of your father's death. 　　聽到您父親逝世的消息 ，令我悲痛不已 。

☆ We are filled with sadness at the news of your daughter's death. 　　令嬡過世的消息 ，使我們非常悲傷 。

☆ I feel sad that there is no way for me to be there *in your hour of need.* 　　在你有需要的時刻 ，我卻無法前去 ，眞令人遺憾 。

---

regret〔rɪˋgrɛt〕*v.* 後悔　　unfair〔ʌnˋfɛr〕*adj.* 不公平的
pain〔pen〕*n.* 痛苦　　sadness〔ˋsædnɪs〕*n.* 悲傷

☺ 給生病中的朋友 ☺

☆ Get well soon！　　　　　　　　　　快點好起來！

☆ *Hurry up and get better.*　　　　趕快好起來。我們需要你。
We need you.

☆ I hope that you are feeling　　　　希望你不久就會覺得好一些。
better soon.

☆ I have prepared a joke book　　　我準備了一本笑話集給你。
for you. These jokes may　　　　這些笑話也許有點陳腔爛調，
be a bit corny and a bit　　　　不再流行了。但我希望它們
past their prime. But I　　　　能逗你開心，消磨時間。
hope they cheer you up and
help pass the time.

☆ While you are in the hospi-　　　當你在醫院時，不要忘了，
tal, always remember that　　　你最好的朋友就是你的護士。
your best friend is **your**
nurse.

☆ *I was sorry to hear that*　　　聽到你生病了，我很難過。
you are sick.

☆ I was so sorry to hear of　　　聽到你病了，我眞是難過。
your illness.

☆ I was shocked to hear that　　　聽說你在醫院裡，我眞是吃
you are in the hospital.　　　了一驚。

---

corny〔ˈkɔrnɪ〕*adj*. 陳腔爛調的

☆ I just can't tell you how sorry I was to hear of your accident.

聽到你發生意外，我真說不出有多難過。

☆ All of us are awaiting your return.

我們都在等你回來。

☆ We hope that you will soon *be up and about*.

我們希望你早日復元。

☆ With every good wish for your swift recovery.

以每一個誠摯的祝福，盼望你迅速痊癒。

☆ With best wishes for your quick and complete return to health.

祝福你早日完全恢復健康。

☆ There are a lot of things that you can do in bed.... but you have to get better first.

在床上,你有很多事可以做…但你得先好起來。

☆ Please *take the time* to give yourself a good rest.

請你讓自己好好的休息。

☆ I was relieved to hear that your sickness is not too serious. But get better just the same.

聽到你的病情不太嚴重，我鬆了一口氣。但你還是得好起來。

---

accident〔'æksədənt〕*n.* 意外事件   *be up and about* 病後復原

☆ I hope you are feeling better.

希望你現在覺得好多了。

☆ I wish that I could visit you in the hospital now.

我但願現在就能到醫院探望你。

☆ *We are all concerned about you.*

我們都很關心你。

☆ This card is from all of us. We hope that you are your same spritely self soon.

這張卡片是我們全體所送的。希望你很快地，又是同樣的生龍活虎。

** ─────────────────

spritely〔'spraɪtlɪ〕*adj.* 活潑的；愉快的

Sample Sympathy Cards

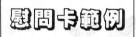

把您的祝福包裝起來

Michael ,
　　Not feeling well ? Here's a
guaranteed way to feel better ….
That's to watch the video tape I
sent you.

　　　　　　　　Edward

參克：

　　不舒服嗎？這裡有一個保證令你痊癒的妙方…。那就是看我送你的錄影帶。

　　　　　　　　　　　愛德華　上

Poor David ,
　　Cheer up ! We know you can
make it, and you never disappoint us !

　　　　The class

可憐的大衛：

　　振作起來！我們知道你絕對辦得到，而你也從不會讓我們失望！

　　　　　　　　　　　全班同學　上

Dear Mike and Nancy,
　　We were shocked to hear of
the death of your father. He will
be missed by all who knew him.

　　　　　Helen and Joe

親愛的麥克和南茜：

　　聽到令尊去世的消息，我們都很震驚。他將會為所有認識他的人所懷念。

　　　　　　　　　　　海倫和喬

** shocked〔ʃɑkt〕adj. 震驚的

Dear Fanny,
　　I feel badly that I can't be
there with you in your time of
mourning. Please send my condo-
lences to the rest of the family.

　　　　Your friend Carrie

親愛的芬妮：

　　在你們悲傷的時候，我很遺憾無法與你們在一起。請代我向家中其他人，致上哀悼之意。

　　　　　　　　　　你的朋友凱麗　上

** mourning〔'mɔrnɪŋ〕n. 悲哀；哀悼　　condolence〔'kɑndələs〕n. 弔慰

Dear Mike,

So sorry to hear that you are sick.
Here are some suggestions for you to
pass the time :

1. Read letters from your friends.

2. Read a medical book and count the
number of symptoms that your have.

3. Look at pictures that you have taken
before.

親愛的麥克：

聽說你病了，實在很難過。這裡有些建
議，可以提供你打發時間：

1. 看朋友的來信。

2. 讀一本醫學的書，數一數你有幾種症狀。

3. 翻一翻從前拍的照片。

** suggestion〔səˈdʒɛstʃən〕 *n.* 建議

4. *Read some lovely comic books like Garfield and Peanuts.*
5. *Think of something that you want to do after you recover.*
6. *Try to remember one of the high school cheer-leaders.*
7. *Write a letter to your doctor and the nurses in the hospital.*

Joe

4. 看一些可愛的漫畫書，像「加菲爾」和「花生米」。
5. 想一想你復原後要做的事。
6. 試著回想高中啦啦隊長之中的一位。
7. 寫一封信給你醫院的大夫和護士。

喬

** symptom〔'sɪmptəm〕*n.* 徵候；病症
cheer-leader〔'tʃɪr,lidə〕*n.* 啦啦隊隊長

Dear Lucy ,

　　The news of your father's death reached us last night. I send my love and deepest sympathy to you and your family. If there is anything that I can do for you, don't hesitate to let me know.

Your aunt ,
Edna

親愛的露西：

　　昨晚我們得知令尊過世的消息。謹向你們及家人致上我的關愛與最深的同情。如有我可以效勞之處，請立刻讓我知道。

妳的姑媽

伊德娜

**　reach〔ritʃ〕 v. 到達

Unit 11 —Encouragement-Cards— 鼓勵卡

≪ Cheer up ! ≫

人生不如意事十之八九。一旦朋友有了困難，或遭遇挫折（*frustration*），一張誠懇的**鼓勵卡**，或許能帶給朋友更多的信心與勇氣來面對失敗。如果是寄給失戀的友人，那你可將這句話送給他或她：" *There are other fish in the sea!* "（天涯何處無芳草！）

😊 事業失敗 😊

☆ I was so sad to hear that your business didn't make it. Hang in there! We all love you.

聽到你商場失意，我很難過。要支撐下去！我們都愛你。

☆ Don't give up hope. It's time to pick up the pieces and *move on to* the next challenge.

別放棄希望。現在該是收拾殘局，迎向另一挑戰的時候。

☆ Try to cheer up. We all support you the same.

試著振作起來。我們還是一樣支持你。

** *cheer up* 振作；快樂起來

☆ At times like these you really
    need your friends. Call me if
    you need anything.

此時你眞的需要朋友。如有
任何需要，打電話給我。

☆ Just try to remember that
    this is not the end of the
    world.

記住這不是世界末日。

☆ We are sorry to hear about
    your business. You are a
    fighter, so just hang in there.

我們很遺憾聽到你生意失敗
的消息。你是個鬥士，要撐
下去。

☆ In these difficult times it
    may seem that all is lost.
    But you still have our love,
    and that is unshakable.

在這困難的時刻，似乎一切
都失去了。但你仍然有我們
永不動搖的愛。

☆ While some things may *pass
    away*, you know that our love
    and affection will not.

世事難料，惟我們的愛和情
感不變。

☆ *This is no time* to think that
    all is lost. You still have
    your family and friends.

此時你不該認爲失去了一切。
你仍然擁有家人和朋友。

☆ I believe that you will start
    anew soon !

我相信你很快將會東山再起！

✱✱────────────

  unshakable〔ʌnˈʃekəbḷ〕*adj.* 不可動搖的
  affection〔əˈfɛkʃən〕*n.* 愛情；感情

☆ We know it's a hard blow to you.

我們知道這對你是個很大的打擊。

☺ 落　榜 ☺

☆ We are sorry that you didn't **pass the exam**. Don't worry, there is always next year.

我們感到遺憾，你沒有通過考試。但別擔心，明年還有機會。

☆ Don't **give up hope**. You can do it, I know you can.

不要放棄希望。我知道你可以做到的。

☆ I know that you have the ability to do it. Don't give up because of this one failure.

我相信你有能力辦到。不要因爲這次失敗而放棄。

☆ You are still tops with us.

你仍是我們之中的佼佼者。

☆ If **at first** you don't succeed, try, try again.

初嚐敗績，再試一次，再試一次。

☆ Don't feel too blue about this. You know, not very many people pass the exam the first time.

不要因此鬱鬱不樂。你知道，能第一次就通過考試的人不多。

☆ You were so close this time. Next time I am sure that you will get it.

這次就差這麼一點。下次你一定會成功。

---

give up 放棄

☆ You made a real good effort.　你眞的盡了力。下次一定可
Next time you are sure to　以上榜。
pass.

☆ There will be many other　成功的路很多，所以，整裝
chances to pass, so *pick*　出發，再試一次。
yourself up by your own
bootstraps and try again.

☆ It is not whether you win or　輸贏並不重要，重要的是其
loose, but how you play the　中的過程。
game.

☆ I know how disappointed you　我知道你現在一定非常難過!
must feel now!

☆ I know that lots of famous　我知道有很多偉人也曾落過
people have failed examina-　榜，但後來他們都繼續努力
tions the first time and lat-　而重考上榜!
er they've done very well!

☺ 失　戀 ☺

☆ Cheer up. *There are other*　快樂些。天涯何處無芳草!
fish in the sea!

☆ Try to cheer up. *All is not*　試著快樂起來。一切都沒有
lost.　失去。

---

pick oneself up 振作起來　　bootstrap〔'but,stræp〕*n.* 鞋帶

☆ Don't think that all is lost. There will be others. You can count on it.

你並沒有失去一切。還有其他機會。好好把握。

☆ It is a far better thing to have loved and lost, than to have never loved at all.

愛過再失去，總比從來沒愛過好。

☆ I know that you are *in pain*, but try to remember that time heals all wounds.

我知道現在你很痛苦，但不要忘了時間能治療一切。

☆ At this time, I know that it is hard to believe, but you will love again.

在此時，很難相信，但你會再度墜入情網的。

☆ If you need a shoulder to cry on, just call. I'll be there in a minute.

如果需要一個可以倚靠著哭泣的肩膀，打電話來。我馬上就到。

☆ Of all of life's pains, this one is perhaps the most painful, but the most fleeting.

在人生的苦痛中，這次也許是最難受的，但也是最短暫的。

☆ It is hard to admit, but perhaps you are the better for it.

或許你很難承認，但也許這樣對你比較好。

---

heal〔hil〕 *v.* 治療
wound 〔wund〕 *n.* 創傷；（信用，名譽，感情等）損害
fleeting〔'flitɪŋ〕 *adj.* 疾逝的；短暫的

☆ No one can ***take away*** what you had.   Just think of the good qualities and consider yourself lucky.

沒有人能奪走你所擁有的一切。往好處想，想想自己是幸運的。

☆ In your present state of mind, I know my words of consolation are futile.

我知道在你目前的心境下，安慰的話是無益的。

☺ 失　業 ☺

☆ ***Don't worry about it.*** You will find a new job before you know it.

別擔心，你很快就會找到新工作。

☆ You will be able to overcome this difficult time, just as you have overcome difficult times in the past.

你會克服這次困難的，就像以前你通過許多難關一樣。

☆ Don't hang it up, hang in there.

別擱在那，要撐在那。

☆ You will be ***on your feet*** in no time.

你很快就會恢復往日的雄風。

☆ He was a no-good boss anyway.

無論如何，他不是個好老板。

---

overcome〔ovə'kʌm〕*v.* 克服；擊敗　　***hang up*** 掛，吊；耽擱
be on one's feet 復元；獨立

☆ No one can predict these kinds of difficulties. Keep a stiff upper lip.

沒有人能預料這種困難。要撐下去。

☆ It was unfair that he asked you to leave after all you had done for the company. I say good riddance.

他要求你離開是不公平的，畢竟你爲公司盡了力。我說呀，離開他們才是大快人心呢。

☆ You are a better man for standing up to the boss, rather than let her walk all over you.

你是個適合做老闆，不適合讓老闆踩在你頭上的人。

☆ *Cheer up*! There are better companies to work for.

快樂些！還有更好的公司等著你去工作。

☆ If you need any help readjusting to your new situation, just call.

如果你對新處境的調適有困難，需要幫助，請打通電話來。

☻ 困 境 ☻

☆ Don't worry too much. Everyone *makes mistakes* now and then.

不要太過擔心。每個人偶而都會犯錯。

---

keep a stiff upper lip 硬撐；堅定不移
good riddance 大快人心，不見了才好
readjust〔͵riə'dʒʌst〕 *v*. 重新調整；適應　　　*now and then* 偶而

☆ Don't take it too hard. These
  things happen *from time to time*.

不要太在意。這種事常發生。

☆ These things happen sometimes.
  Don't let it get you down.

這種事經常發生。不要因此
沮喪。

☆ Don't make it worse than it
  is.

不要把問題愈搞愈糟。

☆ You should give me a call. I
  may be able to help you out.

你該打個電話給我，或許我
可以幫你。

☆ If there is anything I can do,
  just give me a ring.

如果有我可以幫忙的地方，
打個電話給我。

☆ I understand that you are in
  a bit of trouble. If I can
  help, just call.

我知道你有困難。如需要我
幫忙，請打電話給我。

☆ You may be *in trouble*, but it
  is no reason to give up hope.

你或許有麻煩，但不能因此
放棄希望。

☆ Look at the bright side of
  things. You could be in a
  worse situation.

凡事往好處想。你的情況還
不算太糟。

☆ *Every dark cloud has a silver
  lining*.

否極泰來。

** ————————————————

from time to time 有時   *in trouble* 陷於困境；有麻煩
lining〔ˈlɪnɪŋ〕*n.* 鑲邊

☺ 其 它 ☺

☆ If you **make it through** this
then you can make it through
anything.

如果這次你能辦到，天下就
沒有難事了。

☆ I know that you have the for-
titude to make it through
these hard times.

我知道你有勇氣和決心，來
渡過難關。

☆ These hard times make us
strong; they do not destroy
us.

困難使我們堅强；却不能使
我們毀滅。

☆ No man is an island; we all
rely on our friends **in time of**
need.

沒有人是一座孤島；在必要
的時候，我們都得依靠朋友。

☆ It is times like these when
you learn who your friends are.

現在是患難見眞情的時刻了。

☆ We all make flubs, just don't
make the same one twice.

我們都會犯錯，只要不犯第
二次。

☆ **To err is human**; to really
foul things up takes a com-
puter.

人會犯錯，是很自然的；連
電腦都會把事情搞得亂七八
糟。

---

make through 度過　　fortitude〔'fɔrtə,tjud〕 *n.* 堅毅
destroy〔dɪs'trɔɪ〕 *v.* 毀滅；毀壞　　 **in time of need** 在需要的時候
flub〔flʌb〕 *n.* 錯誤　　foul〔faul〕 *v.* 弄髒；搞壞

Sample Encouragement Cards

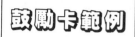

把您的祝福包裝起來

- -

Dear Bob,

A man with your qualifications should have no trouble finding a new job.

Your friend Jeff

親愛的鮑伯：

像你條件這麼好的人才，要找新工作，絕對沒問題。

你的朋友　傑夫上

Dear John,

We all have lost a love in our lives. I know that it hurts but try not to blame yourself too much.

Your sister Linda

親愛的約翰：

在生命中，我們都曾失去所愛。我知道這令人傷心，但也別自責太深。

你的姐姐　琳達

Dear Steve,

　　I heard that you were in some trouble. We all make mistakes sometimes, so don't feel too bad about it. Just be careful not to let the failure dominate your mind too much. I am confident that you will soon start anew to retrieve your loss.

　　　　　　　　Your friend,
　　　　　　　　Annie

親愛的史迪夫：

　　聽說你有了麻煩。我們誰都會犯錯，所以不要覺得太難過。小心別讓這次的失誤佔據了你的心靈。我確信不久你將會東山再起，彌補損失的。

　　　　　　　　你的朋友
　　　　　　　　安妮上

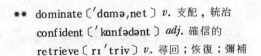

** dominate〔'dɑmə,net〕v. 支配，統治
confident〔'kɑnfədənt〕adj. 確信的
retrieve〔rɪ'triv〕v. 尋回；恢復；彌補

Unit 12 — *Congratulation Cards* —
道賀卡

≪ Congratulations！≫

任何致賀的祝福卡，都不宜拖延。另外，雖然一般書店中的賀卡，都有印上致賀的話，但是親筆書寫，較能帶給對方溫馨的感受。若是道賀他人的 **喬遷之喜**，" *Congratulations on your new house*！"（恭喜您新居落成！）是最常用的祝賀語。

☺ 一般祝賀語 ☺

☆ I am so happy for you.　　　　我真為你感到高興。

☆ I am happy to see that your
many efforts have been re-
warded.　　　　很高興看到你的許多努力，
都有了回報。

☆ Your family must be thrilled.　　你的家人一定非常興奮。

☆ I wish that I could congratulate
you *in person*.　　　　我真希望能親自向你道賀。

☆ I am expecting great things
of you.　　　　我靜候您的佳音。

**

reward〔rɪˋwɔrd〕v. 報答　　thrill〔θrɪl〕v. 使興奮感動
in person 親自地

☆ I hope that your future *is filled with* good fortune.

祝福你，前途一片光明。

☆ This is a great day indeed. Congratulations on a job well done.

這真是個好日子。恭喜你圓滿成功。

☆ You can't believe how proud we all are of your efforts.

你絕不會相信，我們對你的努力，感到多麼驕傲。

☆ This gift is token of our *appreciation* for your efforts.

這份禮物，代表了我們對你所作努力的讚賞之情。

☆ I can't think of anyone who deserves this more than you.

沒有人比你更有資格獲得這項榮譽。

😃 賀昇遷 😃

☆ Congratulations *on* your promotion.

恭喜高升。

☆ You are the one who deserves this promotion.

這次的晉升，你是名符其實。

☆ I can't think of anyone who should have gotten the promotion more than you.

除了你之外，我想不出有誰是更恰當的人選。

☆ Your efforts have really *paid off*. Congratulations !

你的努力真正有了回報。恭喜！

＊＊────────────────

appreciation〔ə'priʃɪ'eʃən〕*n.* 讚賞；感激

promotion〔prə'moʃən〕*n.* 晉升　　*pay off* 有了收獲；得到回報

☆ Way to go ! You deserved it.　做得漂亮！你當之無愧。

☆ Your mother and I are proud
of your achievements.　你的母親和我，對你的成就
都感到十分驕傲。

☆ Congratulations ! Here is the
key to the executive washroom.　恭喜！這是步入主管階層之
鑰。

☆ Don't forget all the little people who helped you *along the
way*. Congratulations !　別忘記過去一路給你扶持的
小人物。恭喜！

☆ I am so happy for you. I knew
that you would do it.　我真爲你感到高興，我早就
知道你會辦到的。

☆ They couldn't have given the
job to a nicer man.　這件差事，他們可再也找不
出更好的人來了。

😊 賀金榜提名 😊

☆ Congratulations on *passing the
exam*.　恭喜你考試過關，金榜提名。

☆ We know that you studied hard.
Congratulations.　我們都知道你很用功讀書。
恭喜了。

☆ Your years of hard work have
paid off. Congratulations !　你的辛苦歲月都有了代價。
恭喜！

☆ We are very proud of you, son.　我們十分引你爲傲，兒子。

**　**————————————

achievement〔ə'tʃivmənt〕*n*. 成就　　washroom〔'waʃ,rum〕*n*. 盥洗室

☆ Passing the exam shows that you worked hard and were serious. | 通過這場考試，表示你用功努力、態度認眞。

☆ You have earned a little rest. Congratulations. | 你贏得了些許的休憩。恭喜。

☆ Not many people achieved this level. Congratulations. | 達到此水準的人，可不多。恭喜。

☆ We think that you are really great. Congratulations. | 我們都認爲你實在很棒。恭喜。

☆ Only the best get ahead, and you are one of them. | 只有最優秀的人才能出頭，而你便是其中之一。

☆ This is something that no one can *take away* from you. Congratulations. | 你的這件成就，沒有任何人能奪走。恭喜。

☺ 賀新居落成 ☺

☆ Congratulations on your new home. | 恭喜您新居落成。

☆ It is a lovely house. Congratulations. | 這房子眞可愛。恭喜。

☆ We can't wait to see the new house. Congratulations on finding such a nice one. | 我們等不及要看新房子了。恭喜你們找到這樣的好房子。

---

ahead 〔 ə'hɛd 〕 *adv.* 在前地

☆ It's the best house *on the block*. Congratulations.

這是街口上最棒的房子了。恭喜。

☆ These flowers are to welcome you into your new house. Congratulations on getting it.

這些花是用來恭喜你們遷入新家的。恭喜喬遷新居。

☆ It will only be a little while before your house becomes a home.

要使你的房子變成一個家，只要一眨眼的功夫。

☆ I can't think of a better house for *a nicer couple* than you. Congratulations and good luck.

我不知道還有什麼好房子，更適合你們這對好夫妻的。恭喜你們，並祝好運。

☆ It is a beautiful house *in* a wonderful *neighborhood*.

這房子真是漂亮，環境也十分優美。

☆ You deserved to have this house. Congratulations!

這棟房子對你再適合不過了。恭喜！

☆ What a beautiful place! Congratulations and best wishes.

多麼優美的地方啊！恭喜並祝福你們。

😊 賀獲獎 😊

☆ Congratulations on winning the prize.

恭喜獲獎。

☆ *You are the best*! Congratulations.

你是最棒的！恭喜。

**

block〔blɑk〕*n.* 兩條街間的距離　neighborhood〔'nebɚ,hʊd〕*n.* 鄰近地區

☆ You are the leader of the pack! Congratulations.　　你是群龍之首！恭喜你。

☆ Congratulations on a job well done. We are proud of you.　　恭喜你順利成功。我們都以你爲榮。

☆ I have always expected and gotten great things from you.　　我一直對你的期望很高，而你也沒有讓我失望。

☆ Your family *is overjoyed with* your accomplishment.　　你的家人對你的成就欣喜若狂。

☆ I have never expected anything but the best from you. Congratulations on winning.　　我對你只有一個期望，就是拿第一。恭喜你獲勝。

☆ This is the thrill of victory. Congratulations!　　這是勝利的激盪。恭喜！

☆ I have begun to think that there is nothing that you can't do. Congratulations.　　我開始要認爲，沒有任何事是你達不到的了。恭喜。

☆ I always knew that you had the qualities of a winner. Congratulations on a job well done.　　我一直都知道你有贏家的本錢。恭喜你順利達成。

＊＊

pack〔pæk〕*n.* 一群；一組　　overjoy〔'ovə,dʒɔɪ〕*v.* 狂喜
accomplishment〔ə'kɑmplɪʃmənt〕*n.* 成就
thrill〔θrɪl〕*n.* 激盪；興奮　　victory〔'vɪktərɪ〕*n.* 成功；勝利

☺ 賀當選 ☺

☆ Congratulations on winning the election.

恭喜你順利當選！

☆ You are the best candidate for the position.

你是這份職位的最佳人選。

☆ *The people know who is the best man.* Congratulations!

人們知道誰才是最優秀的人才。恭喜！

☆ It was a hard fought election and the best man won. Congratulations and good luck.

這眞是場艱困的選戰，而最優秀的人獲勝了。恭喜您，祝您好運。

☆ Congratulations on your appointment to public office.

恭喜你擔任公職。

☆ Best of wishes on your term *in office*. Congratulations.

願你任內，事事順遂，恭喜。

☆ We are proud of your winning the election.

我們爲你的贏得選舉，感到驕傲。

☆ I am so glad that you were elected to the position. *Good luck.*

眞高興你獲得這份職位。祝你好運。

**

election〔ɪˈlɛkʃən〕*n.* 選舉　　candidate〔ˈkændə,det〕*n.* 候選人

appointment〔əˈpɔɪntmənt〕*n.* 職位　　*in office* 在任內

☆ We are expecting great things from you in office. Congratulations!　　　　　　我們都期盼你在任內能有所建樹，恭喜！

☆ I wish I were there personally to congratulate you. Good luck in office.　　　　　　我希望自己能當面向你道賀。祝你任內萬事如意。

😎 賀獲新職 😎

☆ Congratulations on getting your new job.　　　　　　恭喜你獲任新職。

☆ All those weeks of *looking for a job* finally paid off.　　　　　　過去找工作的一切辛勞，終於獲得報償。

☆ Good luck in your new position.　　　　　　祝你工作順利。

☆ They couldn't have given the job to a nicer person.　　　　　　這份工作再適合你不過了。

☆ I guess this means that you will have to go out and buy a whole new wardrobe. Congratulations.　　　　　　我想這表示你得出去添購一些新行頭了。恭喜。

☆ We should get together for a celebration dinner.　　　　　　我們該聚在一起吃頓飯，好好慶祝一下。

＊＊──────────────────

look for 尋找　　　wardrobe〔'wɔrd‚rob〕*n.* 衣櫥

☆ *I guess they recognize talent when they see it*. Congratulations!

我想是他們慧眼識英雄，恭喜！

☆ It must be hard to leave the old company behind, but congratulations on a much better job.

要忘記老公司，不是件容易的事，但恭喜你獲得一份更好的工作。

☆ We will miss you here at the office, but we are happy you found a better job. Congratulations.

辦公室內所有的人，都會懷念你，但我們為你找到一份更好的工作而高興，恭喜了。

☆ It just won't be the same around here without you. But we hope your new job *works out*. Keep in touch.

沒有你，這兒的一切都會改觀。但我們希望你的新工作一切順利。保持連繫。

🤡 賀事業成功 🤡

☆ Congratulations on your successes in business.

恭喜你事業成功。

☆ You have *turned* this company *around*. Congratulations! We all appreciate it.

你使公司有了轉機。恭喜！我們都滿懷感激。

☆ What you have done is superb. Congratulations.

你所做的一切，真是棒極了！恭喜你。

** ────────────────

keep in touch 保持連繫　　superb〔sʊˈpɝb〕*adj.* 極好的

☆ Congratulations on a job well done. You have worked hard for your successes.

恭喜你事業有成。你的成功是由血汗，所換取而來的。

☆ I think that this is a sign of many good things to come from you. Congratulations.

我認爲這是好運降臨到你頭上的一種徵兆。恭喜。

☆ *What you do, you do well.* I have always known that you would reach the top in your field.

不論你做什麼，都能成功。我早就知道你會在你那行裡，出人頭地。

☆ When you do something you do it right. That's why you have succeeded and why we are proud of you.

每回你都能順利完成工作。這正是你之所以能成功，而我們之所以以你爲傲之處。

☆ You have strong abilities and you know how to use them. Congratulations on your recent success.

你能力強，而且知道該如何運用它。恭喜你近日內的成功。

☆ I wish our company had more people like you. *You deserve your success.*

我希望公司裡，能有更多像你這樣的人才。你成功是理所當然的。

☆ All that work was well worth the effort. Congratulations and best wishes for the future.

那樣的一份工作，值得這份努力。恭喜，並祝你鴻圖大展。

＊＊────────────

sign〔saɪn〕*n.* 徵兆

😃 祝賀開幕 😃

☆ Congratulations on your new store !

恭喜你新店開張！

☆ *May the good Lord be with you.* Congratulations on this store.

願幸運之神與你同在。恭喜新店開幕。

☆ Best of luck in your endeavor.

祝你開張大吉。

☆ We wish you good luck and prosperity with your new store.

我們祝你開張大吉，及新店生意興隆。

☆ You have worked hard to *get this started.* I know that you will make a good fortune.

你努力工作，才使得這家店開張。我知道你定會一本萬利，賺大錢的。

☆ This town needs a store like yours. Congratulations and good luck in the years ahead.

這座城市，需要一間像你這樣的店。恭喜並祝開張大吉。

☆ I will be coming by to see your store soon. Good luck and congratulations.

我會很快來拜訪你的新店。恭喜並祝好運。

☆ I am so happy for you and your new shop. I know that it will do well.

我為你和你的新店感到萬分高興。我知道它將生意興隆，財源滾滾。

** ────────────────

endeavor 〔 ɪnˈdɛvə 〕 *n.* 努力　　prosperity 〔 prɑsˈpɛrətɪ 〕 *n.* 興隆
come by 順道拜訪

☆ Everyone in town is talking about your new shop. Good luck in the years ahead.

城裡每一個人，都在談論你的新店。祝你年年好運。

☆ We have gone without a store like yours **for too long**. I have a feeling that it will prosper!

我們已經太久，沒有像你這樣子的店舖了。我有預感它將生生不息，財源廣進！

☺ 賀退休 ☺

☆ Congratulations on your retirement.

恭喜退休！

☆ This is known as the "quality years." Good luck and best wishes.

這是眾所周知的「黃金時期」。祝福你萬事如意。

☆ Now that you have a lot of time on your hands, **what are you going to do**? Congratulations.

你目前既然掌握了充裕的時間，有何打算？恭喜啦！

☆ You have earned your retirement. You have our good wishes and support.

你已經光榮退休了。你擁有我們的祝福和支持。

☆ Congratulations! I know you will **make the best of** these years.

恭喜！我知道你會善用這些時間。

✱✱ retirement〔rɪˈtaɪrmənt〕*n.* 退休　***make the best of*** ~充分利用~

☆ Now you have time to do what you have always wanted to do. Good luck in the years ahead.

現在你有時間，去做自己一直想做的事。願你年年如意。

☆ Retirement is the time for life, not the end of the road. You have many good years ahead of you!

退休不過是人生中的一個階段，而非窮途末路。你還有許多年的美好時光呢！

☆ Retirement is a beginning and a chance to do and see all the places that you want to. Congratulations.

退休就是一個開始，以及可以去做你想做的事，看你想看的地方的時候。恭喜。

☆ You have entered the best time of your life. Congratulations and the best of luck.

你正值一生中的黃金時期。恭喜並祝好運。

☆ We should get together and celebrate this moment. Congratulations!

我們該聚一聚，慶祝這個時刻。恭喜！

☆ Welcome to the world of retirement.

歡迎退休。

☆ It is a time to relax and appreciate all the beautiful things that this world has to offer.

這是個休息和欣賞世界美好事物的時刻。

☆ Enjoy life *to its fullest*!

盡情享受人生吧！

Sample Congratulation Cards

道賀卡範例

把您的祝福包裝起來

Dear Bob,

It was probably one of the most difficult races this year. But you showed character and strength.

Your classmate,
Dick

親愛的鮑伯：

這或許是今年最困難的競賽之一了吧。但你展現了個人的品德和毅力。

你的同學
狄克賀

＊＊ race〔res〕*n.* 競賽

Dear Brook,

You are wonderful. You have turned that company around and pulled it out of the red.

Janet

親愛的布魯克：

你太棒了。你使那家公司有了轉機，並使它不再虧損。

珍娜賀

Dear Joe,

　　You have my sincerest congratulations on your new promotion. I know that you will do well in your new office. Like I said before, this company recognizes talent when they see it. You have an enormous amount of potential in this company. Good luck and best wishes in the years ahead.

　　　　　　　　　　Your sister,
　　　　　　　　　　Emily

親愛的喬：

　　我誠摯地恭賀你的昇遷。我知道你將在新崗位上一展長才。就像我曾經說過的，這家公司慧眼識英雄，你在這家公司中，有著極大的發展潛力。願你好運，並祝年年順遂。

　　　　　　　　　　你的姐姐
　　　　　　　　　　艾茉莉賀

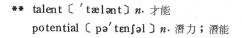

**　talent〔'tælənt〕n. 才能
　potential〔pə'tɛnʃəl〕n. 潛力；潛能

Unit 13 ——Friendship-Cards——
友誼卡

≪ Let's be friends. ≫

友誼（ *friendship* ）是世上最珍貴的寶藏。朋友就像是一本本好書，可以增廣我們的見聞，並給予我們扶持。但友誼却是需要小心維護的，如果你也想伸出關懷的雙手，了解別人的生活，獲得友情的溫暖，請馬上開始寫張卡片，送給身旁的朋友吧！別忘了寫上：" *I am lucky to have you as a friend.* "（我真幸運，能擁有像你這樣的朋友。）

😀 友誼卡常用語 😀

☆ Friendship is a golden gift cherished above all life's treasures.

友誼是一份貴重的禮物，比世上所有寶藏，都更值得珍惜。

☆ I am so glad that we met. Let's try to become closer friends.

我真高興彼此相遇。讓我們試著成為更親密的朋友。

☆ It's wonderful to have you in town. Let's be friends.

我真高興你在這城裡，讓我們做個朋友。

** cherish 〔ˈtʃɛrɪʃ〕 *v.* 珍惜

☆ Let me know if there is anything that I can do for you.

如果有任何我能效勞之處，
請告訴我。

☆ You can count on me as your
close friend.

你可以把我當作知心朋友般
地信賴。

☆ You are a wonderful friend.

你是個很棒的朋友。

☆ *You are my closest friend.*

你是我最親密的朋友。

☆ I was so lonely without you.

沒有你，我會好寂寞。

☆ You are the best friend that
I ever had.

你是我最好的朋友。

☆ I think that we will become
closer through the years.

隨著歲月的逝去，我想我們
會變得更為親近。

☆ Although we got off to a
rocky start, it sure is nice
to have you around.

雖然我們的開始滿佈艱辛，
但有你相伴，真是非常美好。

☆ I feel lucky to have you as
a friend.

有你這樣的朋友，真幸運。

☆ I get by with a little help
from friends like you.

有像你這種朋友的小小協助，
使我度過了難關。

☆ Even though I make mistakes
sometimes, I see that you
are always there for me.

雖然，我有時會犯錯，但我明
白你總是支持我的。

** ————————————————

count on 依賴；信賴　　**even though** 雖然

☆ Thank you for being there *in my time of need*. You are a good friend.

謝謝你在我有需要時，伴隨著我。你真是位好友。

☆ A friend in need is a friend indeed.

患難見真情。

☆ It's nice to know that you will always be there for me.

真高興得知，你永遠支持我。

☆ You know that you can count on me for anything, friend.

你知道你可以凡事信任我的，朋友。

☆ When you are down and troubled, you can count on my love.

當你失意時，你可以仰賴我的關愛。

☆ *Come by and see me* if you need someone to talk to.

如果你需要找個人談談，來看我。

☆ Where would we be without friends?

沒有朋友，我們會是什麼樣呢？

☆ Thank you for being such a good friend.

謝謝你這樣的一位好友。

☆ You were there when I needed you most. Thanks, friend.

當我最需要你時，你總是在那兒。謝謝你，朋友。

☆ Love between friends is often the most enduring kind.

朋友間的愛是最持久的。

＊＊————————————————

enduring〔ɪn'djʊrɪŋ〕*adj.* 持久的

☆ I have never had a friend like you before.

我以前從未有過像你這樣的朋友。

☆ I feel lucky to have met you. You are a great friend.

眞幸運遇見你。你是位很棒的朋友。

☆ Where would I be without friends like you.

如果沒有你這樣的朋友，我眞不知如何是好。

☆ Everything will work out because of friends like you.

有你這樣的朋友，凡事迎双而解。

☆ Thank you for helping me out. I really appreciate friends like you.

謝謝你的幫忙。我眞的很感激有你這樣的朋友。

☆ I *couldn't go on* without friends like you.

若沒有你這樣的朋友，我就無法堅持下去。

Sample Friendship Cards

友誼卡範例

把您的祝福包裝起來

Dear John,

　　You have been such a good friend to me over the years. I just wanted to write a note to tell you that.

Your friend, Nancy

親愛的約翰：

　　你一直是我多年來的好友。我不過是想寫張便條告訴你罷了。

你的朋友南茜　上

** **over the years** 多年來

Dear Bob,

　　It was just a misunderstanding that started us off on the wrong foot. I am glad that is on better terms now. I need a friend like you.

Your friend

親愛的鮑伯：

　　一次誤解使我們有了錯誤的開始。真高興目前情況已好轉。我需要像你這樣的朋友。

你的朋友　上

** misunderstanding〔͵mɪsʌndə'stændɪŋ〕n. 誤解

Dear Jane,

Thank you for helping me out over the past few weeks. It has been tough, but with friends like you, I feel that I can pull through these difficult times. You are so easy to talk to. I thank the good Lord for friends like you.

You know me

親愛的珍：

謝謝你過去幾周的協助。雖然艱辛，但有你這樣的朋友相伴，我覺得自己可以度過這些難關。你是個容易交談的人，感謝幸運之神賜與我像你這樣的朋友。

知名不俱

** tough〔tʌf〕*adj.* 艱辛的
pull through 度過（難關）

Dear Debbie,

　　I didn't want this summer to end. I will remember it for the rest of my life. Don't think of "good-bye" as an ending because in our hearts we will always have a part of yesterday. If you want to talk please just call me. You know that I'm just a phone call away!

　　　　　　　　Your friend,
　　　　　　　　Lucy

親愛的黛比：

　　我真不願意這個夏天結束。我將永遠記得這段日子。別把「再見」當作一種結束，因為我們心中永遠存著昨天的記憶。如果妳想談天，儘管撥個電話，妳知道我們只要一通電話就可見面了！

　　　　　　　　妳的朋友
　　　　　　　　露西上

Unit **14** ───── *Farewell-Cards* ─────

送別卡

≈《 Bon voyage！》≈

朋友將有遠行或將負笈他鄉，你是否也該寄上一張**送別卡**（*farewell card*），祝他旅途平安（*Bon voyage！*）呢？若是寫給即將搬走的鄰居或**轉學**的同學，那麼別忘了加上一句：" *I've cherished the time I spent with you. Keep in touch！* "（我珍惜與你相處的時光。保持連絡喔！）

😊 給遠行的朋友 😊

☆ Bon voyage！

旅途平安！

☆ *Enjoy your trip*！Give us a call when you get back.

祝旅途愉快！回來時打個電話給我們。

☆ Enjoy your vacation！Hope everything goes as planned.

祝假期愉快！希望一切都按照計劃進行。

☆ Have a great time！I wish that I could go too.

好好地玩吧！我希望我也能去。

☆ Have a wonderful trip. I wish I were in your shoes.

祝你有個美妙的旅行。我希望能和你一樣。

** ────────────

bon〔bɔ̃〕*adj.* 法文中的 good「好」之意
voyage〔ˋvɔɪ‧ɪdʒ〕*n.* 陸路旅行；航海

☆ I hope that you get a lot out of your trip！ It sounds very exciting where you are traveling to.

我希望你這次旅行收獲很多！你要去的地方，聽起來很刺激。

☆ *Have a safe trip.* Give us a call when you get there to let us know that you got there *safe and sound*.

祝旅途平安。到的時候，打電話告訴我們，讓我們知道你平安無恙。

☆ I wish that I could go with you. Maybe next time we can go together.

我真希望能和你一起去。下一次或許我們能一塊去。

☆ Best of luck in your brave new world. It's really quite a challenge, but I know that you will do well.

祝你在美麗新世界裡，事事順利。這是一次挑戰，但是我知道，你可以應付得很好。

☆ There is no turning back now！ Best of luck in your new environment.

現在可不能回頭了！祝你在新環境裡，事事如意。

☆ I know that it is hard to write when you are travelling, but drop us *a line or two*.

我知道旅行時，很難寫信，但是請給我們一些隻字片語。

☆ I hope to see you soon and hear all about your trip. *Be careful out there*！

我希望很快見到你，並聽你訴說旅途上的一切。出門在外凡事小心！

---

safe and sound 平安無恙　　**turn back** 折回
environment〔ɪnˈvaɪrənmənt〕*n.* 環境

☆ You have earned this vacation. Enjoy it to the fullest —— no holds barred.

你已經獲得這次假期。盡情地享受——一路順風。

☺ 給搬走的鄰居 ☺

☆ Good-bye！ Don't forget to come back and see us！

再見！別忘了回來看看我們！

☆ I'm so sorry that you are leaving. Let's *keep in touch*！

你要離開了，我眞感到難過。要保持聯絡喔！

☆ " Good-bye " is not an ending when you know that people care, for miles may come between you and I, but warm thoughts are always there.

「再見！」並不代表結束，如果你知道有人在關心你，雖然你我相離千里，但熱情的思念永在。

☆ " Good-bye " is not an ending but a different start for you, a time for making brand-new friends and seeing dreams come true.

「再見！」不是個結束，而是個開始，讓你去結交新朋友，並看到美夢成眞。

☆ " Good-bye " is not an ending, for within your heart you'll always have a part of yesterday.

「再見！」不是一個結束，因爲你的心中一直擁有昨日的一切。

＊＊

barred〔bɑrd〕*adj.* 妨礙的
keep in touch 聯絡　　***come true*** 實現

☆ It is sad to say good-bye, but
I *look forward to* the time when
you and I will be together again.

說再見令人傷感,但是我
盼望你我重逢的時刻。

☆ Thank you for being such a good
friend. I will surely miss your
presence here. Let's keep in touch.

謝謝你一直是我的好朋友。
我一定會想念你在這裡的
一切。讓我們保持聯絡。

☆ It makes me sad to think that we
will be so far apart. Just remember that I am only a phone call
away.

我們相隔那麼遙遠,我真
感到難過。可要記得我們
只要一通電話就可見面。

☆ I have really enjoyed the time we
spent together. It will live on in
my mind *for the rest of my life*.
I promise that I will write to you
often.

我非常珍惜我們一起共度
的時光。我將會永遠記憶
不忘。我保證一定常寫信
給你。

☆ We were neighbors, but now we
will be pen pals. Let me know
how things *turn out* in your new
world !

我們過去是鄰居,但未來
會是筆友。要讓我知道你
在新環境的情形喔!

☆ Take care of yourself ! I will
remember this summer for the
rest of my life. I hope that we
can meet again real soon. Don't
be shy to write.

多保重自己!我永遠都會
記得這個夏天。希望我們
能很快見面。請別羞於動
筆。

---

pen pal 筆友   shy〔ʃaɪ〕 *adj.* 害羞的

Sample Farewell Cards

送別卡範例

把您的祝福包裝起來

Dear Marilyn,

I except to see some pictures when you return. I am a bit envious of you!

Danny

親愛的瑪若琳：

你回來時，我希望能看看你拍的照片。我有點嫉妒你呢！

丹尼上

＊＊ envious〔ˈɛnvɪəs〕*adj.* 嫉妒的

Dear Jim,

Be sure to send us a post card or two. I hope everything goes safe and sound.

Susan

親愛的吉姆：

一定要寄一兩張明信片給我們。希望你一切都平平安安的。

蘇姍

Unit 15 ─ Announcement-Cards ─
通知卡

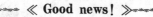

≪ Good news! ≫

一般而言，**通知卡**（ *announcement cards* ）多用在通知**愉快**的消息或事件，如嬰兒誕生、喬遷、或結婚等的通知。至於通知某人的死訊，則多用正式的信函（ *formal letter* ）。在台灣，結婚通知多附帶著婚宴的邀請（ *invitation for a wedding reception* ），需個別註明**婚禮**舉行的地點與**宴客**的地點。

😊 嬰兒誕生通知 😊

☆ An amazing and wonderful act of creation : Amy Lee born November 9, 1988 at 12 : 47 P.M. 8 pounds 9 ounces, 23 inches.

驚人奇妙的創造行動：李艾美於 1988 年 11 月 9 日下午 12 點 47 分出生，重 8 磅 9 盎斯，身長 23 英吋。

☆ Amy Lee, 8 pounds 9 ounces. Born the ninth of November 1988.

李艾美，8 磅 9 盎斯重。生於 1988 年十一月九日。

☆ We want to announce a new addition to our family !

我們要宣佈家中多了一位新成員！

**

amazing〔ə'mezɪŋ〕*adj.* 令人驚奇的

☆ We joyfully announce *the arrival of a baby girl*. Her name is Amy and was born on November 9, 1988.

我們很欣喜地宣佈一位女嬰的降臨。她的芳名是艾美，生於 1988 年十一月九日。

☆ The waiting is over！Pamela delivered a healthy baby girl on the 9th of November.

等待結束了！潘蜜拉於十一月九日生了一個健康的女嬰。

☆ Both mother and daughter are *doing well*. The father, however, is exhausted.

母女均安。可是，父親却累壞了。

☆ The Lee household announces *with joy* the arrival of a baby girl on November 9th of this year.

李家歡喜地宣佈，一位女嬰於本年度十一月九日降臨。

☆ We have a new baby！John Lee was born into our household on November 9th at 12：47.

我們有一個新寶寶！李約翰於十一月九日12點47分加入我們家庭。

☆ The stork has brought us twins！Both are healthy and happy, and mom is doing well.

送子鸛帶給我們一對雙胞胎。兩人都很健康快樂，母親的氣色也很好。

☆ Look what the stork brought to our house：Our lovely Pamela.

看看送子鸛給我們家帶來什麼：我們可愛的潘蜜拉。

** ──────────────

announce〔ə'naʊns〕*v.* 宣佈；聲明
exhausted〔ɪg'zɔstɪd〕*adj.* 筋疲力竭的
household〔'haʊs,hold〕*n.* 家庭；家族   twin〔twɪn〕*n.* 雙胞胎
stork〔stɔrk〕*n.* 鸛（西洋傳說，鸛掌管送子之事）

☆ The Lord has **blessed** this house **with** a healthy baby boy.

上主以一個健康的男嬰，祝福這個家庭。

🔊 搬家通知 🔊

☆ We are moving to Chungshan N. Road, Section 2, Lane 27, 5th Floor #12 Taipei, ROC

我們將搬往，台北市中山北路二段27巷12號5樓。

☆ We have changed our address to: 120 Chungking South Rd., Sec. 1, Taipei, ROC 11041. Our new phone number is: 5110143

我們已經換了新住址：11041 台北市重慶南路一段120號。新的電話號碼是：5110143

☆ **We're moving**! Our new address is: ～ .

我們要搬家了！新住址是： ～ 。

☆ We've recently moved to: ～ 。

最近我們將搬到： ～ 。

☆ So sorry for not letting you know before, but we changed our address to: ～ 。

抱歉沒有早一點讓您知道，我們的住址變更至： ～ 。

☆ The time has come to change locations to: ～ (new address)。

換新居的時間到了： ～ (新地址)。

**

address〔əd′drɛs〕n. 地址
location〔lo′keʃən〕n. 住處；所在

☆ ***Due to*** a job change, we have moved our residence to： ～ .

由於換工作的關係，我們已經遷移住所至： ～ 。

☆ After so many years at our old house, we have finally moved our family to： ～ .

在老房子住了這麼多年後，我們終於搬家到： ～ 。

☆ With the baby ***on the way***, we decided to move into a bigger house. Our new address is： ～ 。

由於小孩即將誕生了，我們決定搬到大一點的房子去。我們的新住址是： ～ 。

☆ We didn't disappear, we just moved. Our new place is： ～ 。

我們沒有失踪，我們只是搬家了。新住址是： ～ 。

☆ Due to ***expanding business*** we have relocated our store at： ～ 。

由於擴大營業，敝店已經遷移至新址： ～ 。

☆ In order to ***serve you better*** we have moved to： ～ .

為了更週到地服務顧客，我們已搬到： ～ 。

☆ We apologize for any inconvenience during this time.

我們為這段期間，對您造成的不便，向您致歉。

** ————————————————

due to 由於 residence〔'rɛzədəns〕 *n.* 住宅；住所
disappear〔,dɪsə'pɪr〕 *v.* 失踪 expand〔ɪks'pænd〕 *v.* 擴充

😊 結婚通知 😊

☆ Mr. and Mrs. Paul Wang request the honor of your presence at the marriage of their daughter Jenny to Mr. John Chen.

王保羅夫婦敬邀您參加他們的女兒珍妮小姐和陳約翰先生的婚禮。

☆ Mr. and Mrs. Paul Wang are delighted to announce the marriage of their daughter, Jenny to Mr. John Chen.

王保羅夫婦欣喜地宣佈他們的女兒珍妮與陳約翰先生的婚事。

☆ The wedding will be held at the St. George Church on Friday, the twentieth of November at seven thirty in the evening.

婚禮將於十一月二十日（星期五）下午7時三十分，假聖喬治教堂舉行。

☆ No gifts are required. RSVP by October thirty-first.

屆時，將不收禮。請於十月三十一日前回覆。

☆ You are cordially invited to attend the wedding of Jenny Wang and John Chen.

誠摯地邀請您參加王珍妮小姐與陳約翰先生的婚禮。

☆ A small reception will be held following the ceremony.

典禮之後，將有小型婚宴。

**
request〔rɪ'kwɛst〕*v.* 懇請　　honor〔'ɑnɚ〕*n.* 榮譽；光榮

delighted〔dɪ'laɪtɪd〕*adj.* 欣喜的　　attend〔ə'tɛnd〕*v.* 參加

☆ Mr. and Mrs. Paul Wang request
the pleasure of Mr. and Mrs. Wu's
company at the wedding of their
daughter.

王保羅夫婦敬邀吳先生夫婦，
蒞臨他們女兒的婚禮。

☆ The ceremony will be held at
St. George Church in Seattle.

婚禮將於西雅圖市的聖喬治
教堂舉行。

☆ It is with great pleasure that
we announce the marriage of our
daughter.

我們很高興地通知您小女的
婚事。

☆ We cordially request your honor
at the ceremony and the reception that follows.

敬邀您蒞臨觀禮，並出席稍
後舉行的婚宴。

Sample Announcement Cards

通知卡範例

把您的祝福包裝起來

· ·

> *Dear Mom ,*
>
>   *It's a girl !*
>
> *Name : Sarah*
>
> *Date : November 9 , 1988 at 12 : 47*
>
> *Weight : 4000 kilograms .*
>
>   *May and Chuck*

親愛的媽媽：

  是位女孩！

姓名：莎拉

生日：一九八八年十一月九日，十二時四十七分。

體重：四千公克。

          玫和查克　上

> *Dear Amanda ,*
>
>   *This card is to inform you that we have changed our residence . We have a wonderful new house here in the city.*
>
>   *Joe*

親愛的艾曼達：

  這張卡片是通知妳，我們已經搬家了。我們在城裡有棟很棒的房子。

         喬

Dear Friends,

We are happy to announce the birth of a girl on the 9th of November. Her name is Amy and she weighs 8 pounds and 9 ounces. She has dark hair and brown eyes and is healthy and happy. Mother is also doing very well. Father, on the other hand, may need a few days to recover.

Lauren & Daniel

親愛的朋友們：

我們很高興地通知你們，我們在十一月九日生了一位女兒。她名叫艾美，重量是8磅9盎斯。她有著黑色的頭髮，棕色的眼睛，很健康，也很快樂。母親的氣色也很好。父親呢，正好相反，也許要靜養幾天才會復原。

蘿倫和丹尼爾

** birth〔bɝθ〕*n.* 出生；誕生
on the other hand 相反地

Dear Aunt Anna,

Dick and I are to be married at Christ Church at noon on Thursday the tenth. We hope you and Uncle George will come to the church and afterward to the reception at the Country Club.

With much love from us both,

Affectionately,
Marilyn

親愛的安娜姑媽：

狄克和我將於十日（星期四）中午在耶穌教堂，舉行婚禮。我們希望您和喬治叔叔，都能到場觀禮，之後並參加在鄉村俱樂部，所舉行的婚宴。

致上我倆對您的愛

愛您的
瑪若琳　上

** afterward〔ˊæftəwəd 〕adv. 之後

Our joy will be more complete
if you can share in the marriage
of our daughter
Sara Chang
to Mr. Joseph Smith
on Sunday, the twelfth of January
nineteen hundren and eighty-nine
at three o'clock in the afternoon
Saint Family Hall
Mr. and Mrs. Alan Chang

張艾倫夫婦謹訂於1989年一月十
二日下午三時，假聖家堂為小女莎拉和
約瑟夫・史密斯先生，舉行婚禮。敬邀
您到場觀禮，一同分享我們的喜悅。

** complete〔kəmˊplit〕*adj*. 完整的

Unit  16 —Welcome-Cards—
歡迎卡

《 **Welcome aboard** 》

如果你家附近搬來一戶**新鄰居**，為了表示你的友好之意，和敦親睦鄰的美德，這時，不妨寫張小卡，問候一下：" *Welcome to the neighborhood* ！"（歡迎搬到這裡來！）若是歡迎**新同學**或**新同事**，你就可以過來人的身分，給他（她）們一些建議或幫忙！

☺ 歡迎新鄰居 ☺

☆ Welcome to the neighborhood! We hope you find it as nice as we do.

歡迎搬到這裡來！我們希望你們和我們一樣喜歡它。

☆ If you need anything, don't hesitate to ask.

如果你們需要任何幫忙，請不要客氣。

☆ We may ask you for a cup of sugar *from time to time.*

我們也許會時常向你們要杯糖。

☆ Congratulations, you have just moved into the best neighborhood in the city.

恭喜，你們剛剛搬進了全市鄰居情誼最好的地區。

---

neighborhood〔'neɪbɚˌhʊd〕*n.* 鄰近地方；鄰居情誼　*from time to time* 時常

☆ Since you picked our neighborhood, we know you have good taste. Welcome！

因為你們選中我們這地方，我們知道你的品味很好。歡迎！

☆ Please *stop by* for coffee. We'd love to get to know you.

請順道過來喝杯咖啡。我們很想認識你們。

☆ We hope you like your new home. You are welcome to bother us at any time.

希望你們喜歡你們的新家。歡迎你們隨時來打擾我們。

☆ We *congratulate* your good taste *on* choosing this neighborhood for your home.

恭喜你們的好品味，選中這個地區當做你們的新家。

😊 歡迎新朋友 😊

☆ It's hard being the new kid on the block. If you need a friend to talk to, just call.

在這一帶當個新人很不容易。如果你需要朋友談談天，只要打電話來找我。

☆ We may all seem like odd-balls and crazy kids, but we're a pretty good bunch of people. *Welcome to the class.*

我們也許看起來都像怪人和瘋狂小子，但是我們是一群好人。歡迎到班上來。

☆ We may look rough and tough, but once you get to know us we're not that bad. Welcome.

我們也許看起來又粗魯又難纏，不過一旦你認識我們，我們並沒有那麼壞喔。歡迎你。

---

taste〔test〕*n.* 品味　　bother〔'bɑðɚ〕*v.* 打擾
bunch〔bʌntʃ〕*n.* 群　　rough〔rʌf〕*adj.* 粗魯的

☆ Our bark is worse than our bite. Welcome to the neighborhood. 　　我們叫得很響，却不會咬人。歡迎到這一帶來。

☆ Welcome to God's country. We hope you like it *as much as* we do. 　　歡迎到上帝之國來。希望你會像我們一樣喜歡它。

☆ You will come to realize that this class is full of crazy kids, but don't let it *scare you away.* 　　你將會發現，這個班上都是瘋狂小子，但是不要讓這事把你嚇跑了。

☆ Welcome to the club! I hope we can be good friends in the future. 　　歡迎加入這個俱樂部！希望我們將來能成爲好朋友。

☆ It must be difficult coming from a foreign country. We will try to make your stay here *as nice as possible.* 　　剛從國外來，必定有適應的困難。我們將會讓你停留在此地，儘可能的舒適。

😊 歡迎新同事 😊

☆ ***Welcome to the firm*.** We know you will do well here. 　　歡迎加入本公司。我們知道你在這裡會表現很好的。

☆ Congratulations on your appointment to the company. If you have any questions *feel free to ask.* 　　恭喜你獲得本公司的職位。如果你有任何問題，請隨時發問。

**

bark〔bɑrk〕*n.* 吠叫　　*scare away* 嚇跑
firm〔fɜm〕*n.* 公司　　appointment〔əˈpɔɪntmənt〕*n.* 職位

☆ Welcome to our company. We should get together for lunch sometime this week to get to know one another.

歡迎到敝公司來。這一週我們該找時間，一起吃個午餐，以便彼此認識一下。

☆ You may feel awkward right now, but I think that you will *fit right in*.

你現在也許會覺得有點不便，不過我想你會進入狀況的。

☆ Don't worry if you make mistakes at first. We all did. Welcome to the firm.

如果你一開始就犯錯了，不要擔心。我們都有過。歡迎加入本公司。

☆ Let's get together sometimes. I would like to get to know my new colleague.

我們有空聚一聚。我想認識我的新同事。

☆ We wish you luck in this firm. We think you have the qualities to *go far*.

祝你在本公司工作如意。我們認為你將會大有可為。

☆ You look like you will fit right in here. We all welcome you to the firm.

看起來你在這裡，會做得很好。我們全體歡迎你加入本公司。

😊 歡迎新室友 😊

☆ I hope my "home sweet home" becomes your "home sweet home."

希望我「甜蜜的家」，變成你的「甜蜜的家」。

**

one another 彼此　　awkward〔ˈɔkwəd〕*adj.* 不便的；笨拙的
colleague〔ˈkɑlig〕*n.* 同事

☆ ***Welcome to the dorm .*** We hope
you like messy roommates ,
loud parties that last all night
and the closest group of friends
in the world . That's just the
way that we are.

歡迎到宿舍來。我們希望你
喜歡生活紊亂的室友，整夜
不停的吵鬧舞會，還有世界
上最親密的一群朋友。我們
就是這樣子。

☆ You couldn't have picked a better room to move into. ***Welcome aboard .***

你不可能找到一個更好的房
間搬進去了。歡迎你搬進來。

☆ Welcome to the house . Don't
be afraid to ask if you need
something.

歡迎搬進來。如果你需要什
麼，請儘管要求。

☆ You can take the bed on the
left . There's food in the fridge
if you are hungry . I'll be home
at 6P.M. Welcome to the house.

你可以使用左邊的床位。如
果你餓的話，冰箱裡有食物。
我下午六點會在家。歡迎搬
進這棟房子。

☆ There's no need to feel uncomfortable. ***Just make yourself
at home .*** Welcome to the dormitory.

不必覺得拘束。請自己隨意。
歡迎搬到宿舍來。

** ──────────────────────

dorm 〔 dɔrm 〕 *n.* 宿舍 (= *dormitory*)

messy 〔 'mɛsɪ 〕 *adj.* 紊亂的

aboard 〔 ə'bɔrd 〕 *adv.* 在壘上；在船上；在飛機上

fridge 〔 frɪdʒ 〕 *n.* 〔俗〕冰箱

uncomfortable 〔 ʌn'kʌmfətəbl̩ 〕 *adj.* 不舒適的

☆ If you like we can go out for pizza and beer tonight. I would really like to get to know you. Welcome to the house.

如果你願意在今晚和我一起出去吃脆餅，喝啤酒。我很想多認識你一點。歡迎搬到這房子來。

☆ If you need anything from a cup of sugar to advice just call on me. *I'll be there.* Welcome to the hall.

如果你需要什麼，從一杯糖到建議，只要叫我一聲，我就會到。歡迎搬到宿舍來。

＊＊

advice〔əd'vaɪs〕*n.* 建議
hall〔hɔl〕*n.* （大學裡的）宿舍；演講廳

Sample Welcome Cards

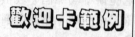

歡迎卡範例

把您的祝福包裝起來

Dear Robert,

  If you like, maybe we could go for a coke or something. Welcome!

Adam

親愛的羅伯特，

  如果你願意，我們可以一起去喝杯可樂什麼的。歡迎你！

亞當

Dear friend,

  Welcome to the class. If you need some help finding your way around school just ask.

Mark

親愛的朋友：

  歡迎到班上來。如果你需要我們幫忙認識學校周圍的路況，只要開口問就可以。

馬克

Dear neighbor,

    All of us in the neighborhood would like
to welcome you to our town. We would like
to get together with you if you have the
time.

David

親愛的鄰居：

　　我們附近的人，都非常歡迎你們搬到我們鎮上。如果你們
有時間，我們想和你們聚一聚。

大衛

Dear Mrs. Lee,

    We know that moving is hectic,
but if you want to take a coffee
break, just give me a call. My number is 7014891.

Mrs. Wang

親愛的李太太：

　　我們知道搬家是很忙碌的，但是如果你們想休息一下，喝
杯咖啡，只要打個電話給我。我的電話號碼是 7014891。

王太太

** hectic〔ˈhɛtɪk〕*adj.* 忙碌的

Dear Daniel,

　　Welcome aboard and congratulations on your appointment. We look forward to working with you here at the firm. The first days can seem kind of rough, but we are sure you will get the hang of it in no time. If there are any problems, don't hesitate to ask. Good luck!

Jane

親愛的丹尼爾：

　　歡迎來本公司，恭喜你獲得這個職位。我們期待在公司中與你一起工作。開頭幾天，也許會有點不順，不過我們確信，你將會很快就掌握訣竅的。如果有任何問題，請儘管發問。祝你好運！

珍

** **look forward to** 期待
　　get the hang of ~ 懂得~的訣竅

Dear new roomie,

Sorry that the room is a mess. I am usually a neat person. I hope you like living here as much as I do. The bed on the left is yours and the closet next to the window is empty. I hope your time here will be happy. Again, welcome!

The one on your right

親愛的新室友：

抱歉房間裡一團糟。我通常是個愛乾淨的人。我希望你和我一樣喜歡住在這兒。左側的鋪位是你的，靠窗的櫃子是空的。我希望你在這兒的時光，會很愉快。再次歡迎你！

睡在你右邊的人

** mess〔mɛs〕n. 混亂

closet〔ˈklɑzɪt〕n. 櫃子

Unit

Graduation Cards

畢業賀卡

≪ **You made it !** ≫

　　畢業（ *graduation* ）是人生中，重要大事之一。在經過了多年的苦讀之後，這就是豐收的時刻了。如果你的好友正要從**醫學院**畢業，那麼，你可以寫 " *I know you will make a fine doctor in the future.* "（我知道你一定會是位好醫生的。）另外，" *Good luck to you everywhere as you journey forth from this graduation day.* "（畢業後，祝福你不論何時何地，好運連連。）

☻ 一般祝賀語 ☻

☆ Congratulations on a job well done !	恭喜你順利完成學業！
☆ Hey ! You made it !	太好了！你成功了！
☆ Way to go ! It was tough, but I always knew you could do it.	做得好！這很難，但是我知道你一定辦得到。
☆ We are very proud of you, son.	兒子，我們以你爲榮！

＊＊

hey〔he〕*int.* 表驚喜詞　　tough〔tʌf〕*adj.* 困難的
proud〔praʊd〕*adj.* 認爲光榮的

☆ Both your mother and I are very proud of you.　　媽媽和我都以你為榮！

☆ *I always knew that you could achieve your goal.*　　我知道你總是能達成目標。

☆ Next stop, College！　　下一站，就是大學了！

☆ I always knew that you had *it* in you.　　我就知道你有這種能力。

😎 給大專畢業生 😎

☆ Now that you've graduated, you still may not know all of the answers.... but you can at least take an educated guess.　　畢業了，雖不代表你能成為萬事通；但至少你可以做有根據的猜測。

☆ Congratulations. We hope you reach the top.　　恭喜。希望你超越顛峯。

☆ Congratulations and good luck in graduate school.　　祝賀你研究所好運連連。

☆ *You've made the most of your outstanding ability.*　　你充分發揮了傑出的才能。

＊＊─────────────

achieve〔ə'tʃiv〕 *v.* 達成　　goal〔gol〕 *n.* 目標
educated〔'ɛdʒə͵ketɪd〕 *adj.* 受過教育的；有經驗憑據的
congratulation〔kən͵grætʃə'leʃən〕 *n.* 恭喜；祝賀
graduate school 研究所　　outstanding〔aʊt'stændɪŋ〕 *adj.* 傑出的

☆ Congratulatinos on your graduation. We're so proud of you.

恭喜畢業，我們以你爲榮。

☆ Your mother and I are real proud.
You've done a fine job, son.

兒子，做得好，媽和我爲你
感到驕傲。

☆ I admire your dedication and
hard work.

我欣賞你的專注與勤奮。

☆ You burned a lot of midnight oil
for four years. Congratulations
on a job well done!

四年來挑燈夜戰。恭喜你完
成一件大事！

☆ *Good luck to you everywhere as*
you journey forth from this
graduation day.

畢業後，祝福你不論何時何地，
好運連連。

☆ May everything that you're hoping
for be yours along the way.

祝你在人生的旅途上，心想
事成，事事順利。

☆ The pain and the struggle ; the
agony and the sacrifice. It was
all worth it, wasn't it ? Congratulations.

所有的辛勞和努力，痛苦和
犧牲，是值得的，不是嗎？
恭喜你。

☆ We were behind you every step
of the way, but you're the one
who did the work. Congratulations.

這一路上我們支持你，但成
功全靠你自己，恭喜。

**

graduation〔,grædʒʊ'eʃən〕 *n.* 畢業　dedication〔,dɛdə'keʃən〕 *n.* 專注
struggle〔'strʌgl̩〕 *n.* 奮鬥；掙扎　sacrifice〔'sækrə,faɪs〕 *n.* 犧牲

☆ You are now a lady of distinction. Good luck in graduate school.

妳現在是位卓越的女性了。祝妳在研究所好運。

☆ *I know that you will be successful in whatever career you choose.*

我知道，不論你選擇哪一行，都是前途無量。

☆ It's a pity that we will be living so far apart. Let's try to keep in touch.

真可惜我們要分開如此遠。讓我們保持連絡。

☆ I will remember these college days with you forever.

我會永遠記得與你大學同窗的日子。

☆ I didn't think that it was possible sometimes, but we both made it! I couldn't have done it without you.

有時我覺得不太可能，但我們成功了！沒有你，我不可能辦到的。

☆ This degree is really something to be proud of.

這個學位值得驕傲。

🌞 給研究所畢業生 🌞

☆ Good luck in the business world with your M.B.A.

祝福你以你的企管碩士學位，在商界大展鴻圖。

**　**

distinction〔dɪˈstɪŋkʃən〕 *n.* 卓越

degree〔dɪˈgri〕 *n.* 學位　　M.B.A 企管碩士

☆ You have mastered a Master. Congratulations on a job well done !

你已經征服了一個碩士學位。恭喜你，幹得好！

☆ Congratulations and good luck in the Doctorate program.

恭喜你，並祝你在博士班順利過關。

☆ *I was going to say some words of wisdom, but I think that you already know them. Congratulations.*

我本想說些哲言，但我想你已經知道了。恭喜你。

☆ Do I have to call you "master", or can I still call you "Big Mouth" ?

我必須稱呼你爲「碩士先生」，還是仍然可以叫你「大嘴巴」？

☆ Congratulations on a superb achievement ! We are all very proud of you.

眞是了不起的成就，恭喜恭喜！我們都以你爲榮。

☆ Now that you are a Doctor, will you be making house calls ?

現在你可是個醫生了，你會到處出診嗎？（ doctor 有醫生和博士之意，此句爲雙關語）

＊＊

Doctorate program 博士課程　　wisdom〔'wɪzdəm〕 *n.* 智慧
achievement〔ə'tʃivmənt〕 *n.* 成就
superb〔su'pɝb〕 *adj.* 極好的；了不起的
make house calls 出診　　master〔'mæstɚ〕 *n.* 碩士

☆ *You've reached the very top of the educational ladder.* Not very many people have done this. Your mother and I are extremely proud of your achievements.

你已經到達教育之梯的最高一階了。不是很多人都能辦到的。你母親和我對你的成就感到非常驕傲。

☆ What an outstanding job you have done! Best wishes in the years to come.

你的成就多麼卓越！在你未來的歲月裡，獻上我最深的祝福。

☆ After all these years of school it is going to be hard thinking of you NOT in school.

經過這麼多年的學校生涯，很難想像你居然不在學校。

☆ *It's time to get a job!* *Good luck!*

是找個工作的時候了！祝你好運！

🙂 給軍校畢業生 🙂

☆ It's over now.　You can stop standing at attention.

訓話完畢。你可以停止立正聽訓了。

☆ Please don't salute your mother when you come home.　Congratulations, son.

回家時，不要也向你媽媽敬禮。恭喜你，我的兒子。

☆ Your mother and I feel proud when we see you in uniform. Congratulations on your successful training.

當我們看到你身著軍服，你媽媽和我都覺得很驕傲。恭喜你成功的受完訓練。

**────────────────

attention〔ə'tɛnʃən〕*n.* 立正　　salute〔sə'lut〕*v.* 敬禮
in uniform 穿上制服

☆ Good luck to you as you look forward from this graduation.

畢業以後，願你步上光明坦途。

☆ *The army has made a man out of you.* We are proud of your achievement, son.

軍隊將你鍛鍊成為一個男子漢。孩子，我們都以你的成就為榮。

☆ You have worked hard and deserve this achievement. Congratulations on a job well done.

你盡了力，這樣的成就名符其實。恭喜你完美地達成任務。

☆ We are all so proud of your fine achievement.

我們對於你這麼棒的成就，都感到非常的驕傲。

☆ *We wish you the best of luck in the years to come.*

我們祝福你，在未來的歲月裡，受到幸運之神最大的眷顧。

☆ Best wishes for the years ahead. You have gotten off to a fantastic start.

願你前程似錦。你已經有了一個奇幻的開始。

☆ Graduation is the time to look back at your past and to your future. Congratulations and good luck in the future.

畢業是回顧以往，展望未來的時刻。恭喜你，願你前途一片光明。

＊＊────────────

army〔'ɑrmɪ〕 *n*. 軍隊　　deserve〔dɪ'zɜv〕 *v*. 應得

proud〔praud〕 *adj*. 驕傲的　　luck〔lʌk〕 *n*. 幸運

fantastic〔fæn'tæstɪk〕 *adj*. 奇幻的　　*look back* 回顧

☺ 給醫學院畢業生 ☺

☆ I guess we can call you "doctor" now. Congratulations on a job well done.

我想現在我們可以稱你一聲「大夫」了。恭喜你順利完成學業。

☆ Now that you've graduated, you can look at my bad back.

既然你現在已經畢業了，來看看我受傷的背吧。

☆ *Congratulations on your graduation from medical school.*

恭喜你從醫學院畢業。

☆ Graduation day.... a fond farewell to yesterday and a warm welcome to tomorrow.

畢業是…向昨日欣然告別，向明天溫馨招手。

☆ It was a struggle, but you made it.

那是一段艱辛的奮鬥，而你却辦到了。

☆ You've just completed one of the first big steps in life. Congratulations.

你已踏出人生中重要的第一步，恭喜你。

☆ *As you look to your future, we stand beside you.* Congratulations on a job well done.

當你展望前途時，我們會隨時在你左右。恭喜你圓滿成功。

** ────────────

farewell〔'fɛr'wɛl, ˏfɛl'wɛl〕*n.* 告別；再會
struggle〔'strʌgl̩〕*n.* 奮鬥；努力

☆ A warm wish for your college graduation.

誠摯地祝賀你大學畢業。

☆ I was wondering if I could be your first patient.

我不知道能不能作你的第一個病人。

☆ As your father and your advisor, *I wish you good luck in the years to come.*

身為你的父親兼顧問,我祝福你在未來的日子裡一帆風順。

**────────────────

advisor〔əd'vaɪzɚ〕 *n.* 顧問

Now that you've graduated, you still may not know all the answers...

Sample Cards for Graduation

畢業賀卡範例　　　　把您的祝福包裝起來

Mark ,

　　Boldly, you defy a thousand pointed fingers. But like the ox, you bow before the children. You did well. Congratulations.

　　Your best friend Johnson

馬克：

　　你曾多次公然地反抗世俗的指責，卻像謙遜的牛一般，執著於赤子的純真。做得好。恭喜你了。

　　　　　　　你的摯友強生

** defy 〔dɪˈfaɪ〕 v. 反抗

My Dear Pearl ,

　　Your years of hard work finally paid off. Continued progress in the years ahead.　　*Your sister , Annie*

我可愛的珍珠：

　　辛苦總算有收穫。祝你往後的日子，百尺竿頭，更進一步。

　　　　　　妳的姐姐　安妮上

Dear son,

Your mother and I are very proud of you on this day. You have worked hard for this degree. You deserve special recognition for your fine achievement. We are behind you 100 % in your career goals. Good luck in the future !

Your Dad

親愛的兒子：

這一天，我和你媽都以你為榮。為了這個學位，你曾如此努力過。你的成就值得肯定。我們對你的生涯目標，百分之百地支持。祝你好運！

你的爸爸

** recognition〔͵rɛkəgˈnɪʃən〕*n.* 認定；肯定

Dear Paul,

   We made it! After all those sleep-
less nights studying for the exams. I
think I need a month of sleep to make
it all up. You have been a great study
partner and a good friend throughout
these last two years. I know you will
make a fine doctor in the future. Let's
keep in touch through the years.

                    Your good friend

親愛的保羅：

   在無數個苦讀應戰的夜晚之後，我們都
做到了！我想我需要睡上一個月，才補得過
來。在最後的二年當中，你曾是我最好的讀
伴與朋友。我知道你一定會是個好醫生的。
讓我們一直保持聯絡吧。

                    你的好友　上

   ** *make up* 補充；補償

||||||||||||| ●學習出版公司門市部● |||||||||||||||

台北地區：台北市許昌街 10 號 2 樓 TEL：(02)2331-4060・2331-9209
台中地區：台中市綠川東街 32 號 8 樓 23 室
　　　　　TEL：(04)2223-2838

||||||||||||||||||||||||||||||||||||||||||||

卡片英語

編　　著 / 陳怡平
發 行 所 / 學習出版有限公司　　　　☎ (02) 2704-5525
郵 撥 帳 號 / 0512727-2 學習出版社帳戶
登 記 證 / 局版台業 2179 號
印 刷 所 / 裕強彩色印刷有限公司
台 北 門 市 / 台北市許昌街 10 號 2 F　　☎ (02) 2331-4060・2331-9209
台 中 門 市 / 台中市綠川東街 32 號 8 F 23 室　　☎ (04) 2223-2838
台灣總經銷 / 紅螞蟻圖書有限公司　　☎ (02) 2795-3656
美國總經銷 / Evergreen Book Store　　☎ (818) 2813622
本公司網址　www.learnbook.com.tw
電 子 郵 件　learnbook@learnbook.com.tw

售價：新台幣一百八十元正
2002 年 5 月 1 日一版六刷

ISBN 957-519-317-2